Speaking of
Ayurvedic Remedies

This book is a handy, up-to-date and authoritative guide to the practice of Ayurveda, the Science of Living, believed to have been imparted by Brahma, the Lord of Creation. It contains time-tested remedies for the treatment of common diseases including jaundice, rheumatism and skin infections for which only Ayurveda provides a complete cure. These are home remedies which cost little, have no side-effects or allergic reactions unlike allopathic medicines, and are within the reach of all. Combined with diet and regimen, they not only cure ailments, but also promote health and longevity.

Dr. T.L. Devaraj, born in 1938, graduated in Ayurveda from the Government College of Indian Medicine, Mysore, in 1963. He was deputed for higher studies in Ayurveda to Banaras Hindu University (D.Ay.M.) in 1972. He has worked as an Ayurvedic Physician, as a Health Officer and as Assistant Professor and Professor at the Government College of Indian Medicine, Bangalore. He is working as Principal at Taranath Government Ayurvedic College, Bellary, Karnataka State.

Dr. Devaraj is the author of several books and research articles on Ayurveda. He received international service award for his contribution to Ayurveda.

Your Health Guide Series

Speaking of CHILD CARE & NUTRITION
Dr. M. Raheena Beegum

Speaking of SKIN CARE
Parvesh Handa

Speaking of AYURVEDIC YOGA AND NATURE CURE
Dr. T.L. Devaraj

Speaking of AYURVEDIC REMEDIES
Dr. T.L. Devaraj

Speaking of CHILD CARE
Dr. Suraj Gupte

Speaking of NATURE CURE
K. Lakshmana Sarma & S. Swaminathan

Speaking of AYURVEDIC HERBAL CURES
Dr. T.L. Devaraj

Speaking of DIABETES AND DIET
Dr. Deepa Mehta & Dr. S.A. Vali

Speaking of YOGA
Pandit Shambhu Nath

Speaking of YOGA AND NATURE-CURE THERAPY
K.S. Joshi

Speaking of YOGA FOR HEALTH
INYS

Speaking of EATING FOR A HEALTHY LIFE
Deepa Mehta

Speaking of SLEEPING PROBLEMS
Dietriech Langen

Speaking of HEART ATTACKS
Carola & Max. J. Halhuber

Speaking of ASTHMA
Dietrich Nolte

Speaking of HIGH BLOOD PRESSURE
Hanns P. Wolff

Speaking of FITNESS OVER 40
Dr. Walter Noder

Speaking of
Ayurvedic Remedies

Dr. T. L. Devaraj

NEW DAWN PRESS, INC.
USA• UK• INDIA

NEW DAWN PRESS GROUP

Published by New Dawn Press Group

New Dawn Press, Inc., 244 South Randall Rd # 90, Elgin, IL 60123
e-mail: sales@newdawnpress.com

New Dawn Press, 2 Tintern Close, Slough, Berkshire, SL1-2TB, UK
e-mail: sterlingdis@yahoo.co.uk

New Dawn Press (An Imprint of Sterling Publishers (P) Ltd.)
A-59, Okhla Industrial Area, Phase-II, New Delhi-110020
e-mail: info@sterlingpublishers.com
www.sterlingpublishers.com

Speaking of Ayurvedic Remedies
© 2005, Dr. T.L. Devaraj
ISBN 1 84557 029 4
.Reprint 2006

PRINTED IN INDIA

FOREWORD

I am happy to go through this valuable book on Ayurveda, entitled *Ayurvedic Remedies for Common Diseases*, written by Dr. T.L. Devaraj.

Dr. Devaraj is a scholar in Ayurveda who has gained wide popularity not only as an Ayurvedic physician but also as a writer of books on Ayurveda. His book, *The Panchakarma Treatment of Ayurveda* in English and *Panchakarma Chikitsa Vijnana* in two volumes in Kannada, won him appreciation from many authorities on Ayurveda. He has got many firsts to his credit. He has also written a book, *The Health and Family Welfare in Ayurveda,* and a booklet on family planning in ancient India, both in Kannada. These books are the first of their kind in the English and Kannada languages. His book, *Mane Maddu* (home remedies) in Kannada has received appreciation not only from Ayurvedic physicians but also from the Karnataka Government which has sanctioned for it a token grant of Rs. 2,000.

Dr. Devaraj has published several research papers on Ayurveda. His great works have won appreciation from eminent scholars of Ayurveda. He was honoured by His Holiness Jagadguru Shankaracharya of Sringeri Mutt, Karnataka State, for his outstanding contribution to Ayurveda.

In the present work, Dr Devaraj has tried to prescribe Ayurvedic remedies for diseases of which allopathic names are mentioned. It is easy for the common reader to follow the Ayurvedic line of treatment as most of the medicines required are easily available and have no side-effects. Even to today, there are diseases like jaundice, rheumatism, skin infections, etc., which require only Ayurvedic treatment for a complete cure. India is proud of this system of medicine which has been rejuvenated since the dawn of Independence.

The author has also recommended diet and regimen to be followed during treatment.

Photographs of plants (drugs) given in the book will help the readers to identify and use them.

The book is useful for the layman as well as medical practitioners and foreigners interested in Ayurveda.

Dr. Devaraj deserves hearty congratulations for having brought out this useful book, written in lucid style.

May Lord Dhanwantari bless Dr Devaraj and enable him to bring out more works on this subject for the benefit of the suffering humanity and to spread knowledge of this science among the medical community of the world and to educate the public about the utility and efficacy of Ayurveda.

<table>
<tr><td>Deputy Director,</td><td>Dr.Venkata Naik</td></tr>
<tr><td>Health and Family Welfare Services,</td><td>M.B.B.S., M.D., D.P.H.</td></tr>
<tr><td>Directorate of Health Services,</td><td></td></tr>
<tr><td>Bangalore 560009</td><td></td></tr>
</table>

PREFACE

Modern medicine consists mostly of antibiotics and chemo-therapeutic drugs, which are employed to kill the bacteria responsible for production of disease. These drugs kill not only pathogenic bacterias but also becterial flora which is considered essential for the maintenance of health and longevity. Moreover, their prolonged use makes the pathogenic bacterias resistant to these drugs. They also produce serious side-effects and interfere with the metabolic process of the body, causing more and more diseases, and producing various types of allergic reactions.

Thus, there is an urgent necessity for an alternative and effective system of medicine, which not only cures diseases, but also preserves and promotes health. In this field, Ayurveda continues to play a prominent role. It increases the resistance of the patient without producing any side-effects.

The diseases discussed in the book are given their allopathic names, so that those conversant with the terminology of modern medicine can easily follow the line of Ayurvedic treatment.

The book mentions the causes and symptoms of diseases according to Ayurdeva and prescribes the treatment for them. Most of the drugs used are home remedies which are within the reach of everybody. Standard Ayurvedic preparations manufactured by drug comppanies are also given.

The book is written mainly for the layman, as well as foreigners and practitioners of different systems of medicine like Allopathy, Ayurveda and Unani. It is beyond the scope of this book to give descriptions and procedures of manufacture of the drugs mentioned in the book. Most of the common diseases are dealt with in the book and their treatment given along with diet and regimen.

Dr T.L.Devaraj

ACKNOWLEDGEMENTS

I am highly indebted to Dr Venkata Naik, M.B.B.S.,M.D.,D.P.H., Deputy Director of Family Welfare Services, Directorate of Health and Family Welfare Services, Karnataka State, for his valuable Foreword to the book.

I am much obliged to Professor S.M. Angadi of the Post-graduate Department in Dravyagunas and Rasa Shastra, and Dr. S.I. Ahmed, Professor and Principal, Government Unani Medical College, Gulbarga, Karnataka State, for their useful comments on the book.

I am grateful to Dr. K.R. Srikanta Murthy, Principal, Government College of Indian Medicine, for the constant encouragement he gave me.

CONTENTS

Foreword   v
Preface   vii
Acknowledgements   viii
1.   Ayurveda   1
2.   The Digestive System: Diseases and Remedies   8
3.   The Respiratory System: Diseases and Remedies   32
4.   Cardio-Vascular and Haemopoetic Systems: Diseases
     and Remedies   42
5.   Fevers and Their Remedies   52
6.   Genito-urinary System: Diseases and Remedies   66
7.   Metabolism and Glands: Diseases and Remedies   86
8.   Skin and Hair: Diseases and Remedies   93
9.   Nervous System: Diseases and Remedies   100
10. Eye, Ear, Nose and Throat: Diseases and Remedies   108
11. Rheumatic Arthritis and its Remedies   118
     Medicinal plants quoted in the book   120
     Major manufacturers of Ayurvedic medicines
     and formulations in India   131
     Index   132

MY VIEWS

I have gone through the book *Ayurvedic Remedies for Common Diseases* written by Dr. T.L. Devaraj, who is a good writer of books and articles. He is a very enthusiastic man of progressive mind and high aspirations. In this book he has dealt with the etiology, pathogenesis of the diseases in brief and mentioned the simple Ayurvedic remedies with dietic regimen for every disease. This book would be useful for the students, general practitioners of Ayurveda and the practitioners of other medical systems who are interested to know about Ayurvedic treatment for the various common disorders.

B.A., D.S.A.C., H.P.A.   **Dr. S.M.Angadi**
Professor & Head of the Dept. of P.G Studies
Govt. College of Indian Medicine, Bangalore-560 009

OPINION

Dr.T.L.Devaraj is an outstanding academician, a learned scholar and a prolific writer. He has brought out the book *Ayurvedic Remedies for Common Diseases* to fulfil the needs of the time. It is a step forward to solve our national problem regarding health. The common diseases and the remedies are dealt with in a very simple and lucid style. It is in the fitness of things that books of this type should be brought out to fulfil the longstanding lacuna. I feel myself proud of offering my comments on such an outstanding work. I hope this work will receive wide commendation and appreciation from the scholars, teachers and students and practitioners of Allopathy and Ayurveda, and prove beneficial in solving the 'National Health Problems'.

Professor & Principal   **H. Syed Ishtiaq Ahmed**
Govt. Unani Medical college
Gulbarga
Pin: 585 101
Karnataka State

1

AYURVEDA

'Ayurveda' consists of two words: Ayu and Veda. It is a Sanskrit term and it literally means the science of life. The scope of Ayurveda is vast. It not only deals with the prevention of diseases and promotion of health and longevity but it also cures the diseases. Ayurveda also deals with rejuvenation. Ayurveda can also be called the Science of Living and it is Upaveda (Supplementary Veda) of the Atharva Veda. According to the Shastras the knowledge of Ayurveda was imparted to Daksha Prajapati by Brahma, the creator of the universe. Knowledge of Ayurveda then descended to two Ashwini Kumaras and later on to Lord Indra. Dhanwantari was sent by Lord Indra to earth to propagate the knowledge of Ayurveda to the others. Sushruta was the student of Dhanwantari, who wrote the famous treatise on surgery entitled *Sushruta Samhita*. Charaka was the contemporary of Sushruta who wrote a book on Medicine entitled *Charaka Samhita*. Ayurveda has eight branches. They are as follows:

1. Kayachikitsa   (General Medicine)
2. Shalya   (Surgery)
3. Shalakya   (Treatment of Diseases of Head, Neck including Eye & E.N.T.)
4. Graha Chikitsa   (Psychotherapy)
5. Damstra Chikitsa   (Toxicology)
6. Bala Roga Chikitsa   (Paediatrics)
7. Jara Chikitsa   (Rejuvenation)
8. Vrishya Chikitsa   (Aphrodisiacs)

The universe is composed of Pancha Mahabhootas or five basic elements, viz., Prithvi, Ap, Tejo, Vayu and Akasha or Earth, Water, Fire, Air and Ether respectively. The human body is also made up of the above pentads of substances. So there is a natural harmony between the universe and man according to Indian philosophy and Ayurveda.

The Theory of Tridoshas

Ayurveda mainly believes in the theory of tridoshas: Vata, Pitta and Kapha; Vata is powerful force in the body which is produced due to the combination of two elements of the universe, Vayu and Akasha Bhootas. Kapha is produced due to the predominance of Prithvi and Ap Bhootas (Earth and Water). Pitta is produced due to predominance of Tejas. According to Ayurveda there are seven types of dhatus or tissues. The constitution of an individual is also dependent upon tridoshas and the predominance of one type of dosha will decide the constitution of an individual. For example, if an excess of vata is present in an individual, then his constitution will become vataja; so also it holds good in pittaja and kaphaja constitutions. Every type of constitution will have a separate type of diet and habits.The method of treatment depends upon the type and constitution of an individual.

Ayurveda treats an individual as a whole and not only the symptoms of the affected parts, unlike modern medicine. Disease is produced due to imbalance in the normal state of equilibrium of tridoshas. The doshas will govern the physiological activities of the body, and dhatus are produced due to the intake of food. The malas are substances which are formed in the body, and a portion of them may be thrown out; the remaining may be absorbed and helps in the physiological functions of body tissues. Any derangement in the state of equilibrium ih the body will create an healthy atmosphere, for the growth and multiplication of bacteria. Ayurveda also believes in the production of the germs and their disease-producing process. The Ayurveda pleads that the disease is produced mainly due to the imbalance of tridoshas.

Diet: The regimen of diet is more important than medicine in Ayurvedic systems of medicine.

Pathyesathi Gadarthasya Kimaushadha Nishevanam

Pathya Asathi Gadarthasya Kimoushadha Nishevanam

There is no need for medicine if one takes proper food and adopts a proper regimen. One must take the medicine with a suitable diet and proper regimen as advocated in the line of treatment. There is no meaning in taking treatment without a proper diet.

Diet plays a prominent role in regulating the health of an individual. When the body, mind and soul are in equilibrium and functioning properly, such a state is called health. When this natural state comes in contact with an imbalanced state, unhappiness is nothing but a disease.

The main aim of an Ayurvedic physician is to restore the imbalanced state of doshas to their normal healthy state.

Dosham Dooshyam Balam Kalam Analam, Prakritim

Vayaha Satvam Satmyam, Tathaharam

Avasthaschapritakvidha

Sookshma Sookshmam Parikshesham Dosaushadha

Nirupane Yo vartate chikitsayam, Nasaskalati Jathujith

Ayurveda takes into account the vitiation of vata, pitta, and kapha doshas, age of the patient, environment, strength, power of tolerance, season of ailment in question, the power of digestion, mental state, the habit and idiosyncrasies, the food usually taken and other minute terms related to the patient, all these in determining the morbid condition and deciding the line of treatment; then only actual treatment will be instituted and never fails in its task.

Diagnosis: 1. Interrogation of patient
2. Objective examinations
3. Examination by inference or indirect method.

The patient is examined as a whole depending upon his bodily constitution and physical build, psychic development, compactness, proportion of the body, capacity of the gastric fire, capacity to do exercise, and age. The physician has to take the case history in detail and ascertain the type of constitution of the patient.

Firstly, the doctor will ascertain the past history of disease of the patient or his family. Next he will move to the next stage of examination of nails, eyes, nose, lips, teeth, tongue, hands, feet, hair, pupils, faeces, and colour of the body. Thirdly, he will go to the stage of palpating the body of the patient to ascertain whether it is normal. Fourthly, the physician will go on to the next stage of examining the particular organ or entire body for the following signs and symptoms: moist and dry, cold and hot, rough or smooth and rigid or loose.

Later on, the physician will find out the bad odour and listen to sounds produced in different organs.

The next stage of examination is to diagnose the disease by inference, on the basis of his interrogation of the patient and the examination which he has already finished. Thereafter only he will be able to conclude the type of doshas responsible for the disease. In Ayurvedic books there is a detailed description available about the increase and decrease of doshas. These doshas will be either aggravated, and moved to some other place or get lodged in that place and produce the symptoms of the disease. The physician of Ayurveda must also study the state of body fluids, blood, flesh, fat, bone, marrow, semen and the vital essence of body called Ojus. It is also called vital force. Charaka says that the physician can differentially diagnose curable and incurable conditions, and start treatment with a good degree of success. A person who has the equilibrium of tridoshas, dhatus, and agni and who is happy in body, mind and spirit is termed as a healthy person.

"Samadosha Samagnischa Samadhatu Malakriyaha
Prasannatmendriyua Manaha Swastha Ityabhideeyate"

(S.Su.15/41)

In addition to the above examination and investigations Ayurvedic seers like Bhavamishra and Sharangadhara have opined in their *Bhawaprakash* and *Sharangadhara Samhitas* a detailed description of the examination of the pulse to detect the disease. In addition to the examination of urine, stools, sputum, skin, tongue and voice, the diagnosis of the disease can be made only by reading the pulse. With this one can ascertain whether vata, pitta and kapha are aggravated and produce a disease. In addition to the above, the digestive power of the patient will indicate some diseases.

Causes for the Production of Disease

Enough has already been written about the somatic doshas, namely, vata, pitta and kapha. The normal functioning vata is of prime importance among the other doshas in the body. It controls all functions of the body and mind including the doshas, pitta and kapha. It is just like the air of the universe.

The normal vata is of five kinds, viz.,

1. Prana
2. Udana
3. Vyana
4. Samana
5. Apana

Prana vayu is a source of life, without which one cannot live, and which is also responsible for swallowing food and breathing, spitting, sneezing and belching. It not only regulates the heart and other vital organs including the senses of the body, but also makes them work life-long. *Udana vayu* is the main source for the strength of the body and mind. It moves from the nose up to the umbilicus and it is also responsible for the production of various sounds. The strength of the mind and its fûnctions, like memory and intellect and speech, are controlled by it. Colour, strength, memory and courage are controlled by it as well. *Vyana vayu* is situated in the heart and moves all over the body. It carries the rasa (food juice) and blood throughout the body and nourishes the entire system of the body. It not only helps in the opening and closing of the eyelids and other movements of the body, but it also aids in the secretion of perspiration. *Samana vayu* is situated near the digestive fire and moves all over the alimentary tract. It helps in the digestion, assimilation and differentiation of food from nutrient and excreta, and propels the contents of the intestines forward. In other words, it controls the digestive fire and enzymes which are secreted in the gut. *Apana vayu* is situated in the lower part of the digestive tract and it moves in the pelvis, bladder and external genitalia. It helps in the expulsion of urine, faeces, flatus and foetus, menses and semen.

There are five types of pitta, namely:

    a. Pachaka
    b. Ranjaka
    c. Sadhaka
    d. Bhrajaka
    e. Alochaka

Pachaka pitta is situated in between the stomach and the intestines and it is mainly responsible for the digestion of the food that we eat. It can be correlated to digestive juices, hydrochloric acid and enzymes secreted in the stomach and small intestine. It also regulates the functions of other pittas in the body.

Ranjaka pitta gives colour to the food juice before it goes from the stomach to the liver. *Sadhaka pitta* is situated in the heart and helps in the normal functioning of the mind and its activities. It helps in acquiring knowledge and memory. *Bhrajaka pitta* is situated in the skin and regulates the tint of the skin. *Alochaka pitta* is situated in the eyes and is mainly responsible for regulating the normal vision, size and colour of objects.

Like vata and pitta, the kapha is also of five types, viz.,

    a. Kledaka
    b. Avalambaka
    c. Bhodhaka
    d. Tarpaka
    e. Sleshaka

Kledaka kapha is situated in the stomach and helps in moistening the food in the stomach. It nourishes other kaphas.

Avalambaka kapha is situated in the tongue and aids in detecting the taste of food which is swallowed. Thus its place is from the root of the tongue to the throat. It helps in increasing the appetite. *Tarpaka kapha* is situated in the head and cools the eyes and nose. *Sleshaka kapha* is situated in the joints of the body, and it helps them to function properly.

In addition to the above elements, Ayurveda has given importance .o another element, namely Agni. Its main function is to digest the food with the help of samana vayu and kledaka kapha. There are 13 types of Agnis in the body of which seven are dhatvagnis (7 tissue enzymes), five bhootagnis and one Jatharagni (digestive fire in the stomach). The agni is otherwise called pitta (Pachaka pitta). It is very important for the promotion of the health of an individual.

The food that we take will be digested by the factors mentioned above producing six types of rasa (sweet, sour, salty, pungent, astringent and bitter). The food will be acted upon by Bhodhaka kapha in the mouth and Kledaka kapha in the stomach. The digested food will ultimately lead to Madhura vipaka (sweet digestive juice) and later on it will be acted upon by pitta. Then the digestive fire will dry up the waste products and propel them into the large intestines. Rasa can be produced from cereals, fruits and flesh. It may be noted here that each and every drug of Ayurveda consists of one or a combination of six rasas. Important constituents of our body, i.e., dhatus, are seven in number.

1. Rasa   (Chyle)
2. Rakta   (Blood)
3. Mamsa   (Flesh)
4. Meda   (Fat)
5. Asthi   (Bones)
6. Majja   (Bone Marrow)
7. Shukra   (Semen)

In addition to the doshas and dhatus already explained the other important factors are malas (excretory secretions). The important malas are mala (faeces), mootra (urine) and sweda (sweat). These are produced as end products of digestion and excretion from tissues, for example, kapha is the by-product of rasa, and, other malas are pitta, mootra, pureesha, prajanana mala, sweda. 'Kha' malas are secretions from the ear, nose, and mouth, etc.

The Ayurvedic line of treatment mainly aims at the removal of the doshas from their origin or mulasthana (place of origin) in order to eradicate them totally. So it is necessary to know the pathogenesis of the disease and its site of origin.

Most of the diseases are produced due to 'ama' (an uncooked or undigested material). It is due to indigestion. It acts as a toxin or allergin and circulates all over the body producing all types of symptoms. Diseases are spread through the blood and other fluids 'Shakhanusari' and some diseases are spread through the gastro-intestinal and respiratory tract called 'Kosthanusari'. Some other diseases are spread through vital organs, bone and joints called "Marmashthi-Sandhyanusari". The site of manifestation of diseases is in dhatus or blood vessels and lymphatics. There are some diseases produced with the causative factors of stomach called "Amashayodbhava", for example, Amavata (Rheumatic disease). Diseases which are produced due to the impairment of the large gut are called "Pakvashasyodbhava". Pakvashya is nothing but the distal end of the intestines through which the waste products of food are thrown out. The irregular intake of food leads to many diseases right from simple constipation to complicated colitis and cancer.

It is evident from the details given above that Ayurveda has laid more emphasis on the origin of the diseases, the course of their spread and their manifestations. It is mainly dependent upon the predominance of doshas.

Drugs used in the treatment of diseases also have the same type of actions on the fundamental causative factors, viz., Tridoshas. These drugs are mostly non-toxic and act as tonics and not only prevent the diseases but also cure them. Diseases are produced due to psychosomatic causes. Hence, there is an interrelation and interdependence between the mind and body. Medicine, diet and regimen are prescribed by taking all these into account.

2

THE DIGESTIVE SYSTEM
Diseases and Remedies

In *Charaka Samhita Chikitasthana* (15th chapter), the characteristic features of Agni are described as follows:

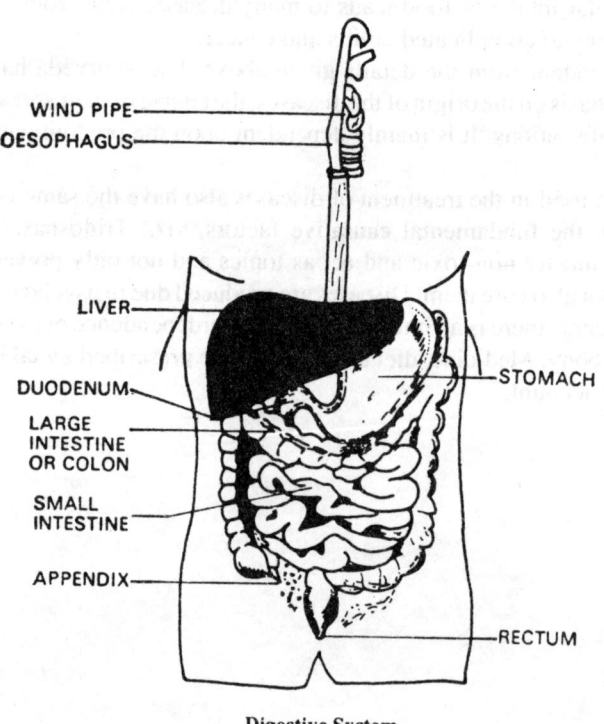

WIND PIPE

OESOPHAGUS

LIVER

DUODENUM

LARGE
INTESTINE
OR COLON

SMALL
INTESTINE

APPENDIX

STOMACH

RECTUM

Digestive System

The lifespan, complexion, vitality, good health, zest, plumpness, glow, vital essence, lustre, heat and the life breath are all maintained owing to the presence of proper Agni in the body. Its proper maintenance is essential for the promotion of good health. Before the subject of digestive disorders is dealt with, it is necessary to know the process of digestion. The stomach is one of the important organs of the body, necessary for the purpose of digestion and the assimilation of food which one consumes. As a result of this process the body will be nourished. The stomach is not only a storehouse of food, but it also makes it more permeable through the different types of juices it secretes. The inner lining of the stomach is covered with mucous membrane consisting of small glands which secrete hydrochloric acid and enzymes. There are two ferments, namely, renin and pepsin, present in the stomach juice which will help the food to break down into smaller particles or molecules. The hydrochloric acid also aids in the hydrolyses of the food that we take. The food which we consume is acted upon by bile juice, pancreatic juice, intestinal juice and lastly, bacteria. These juices will break the food down into smaller particles amenable for absorption. The water is absorbed in the large intestines and the residual food passes through the bowels as a small mass. This is, in short, digestion according to the modern system of medicine.

The Ayurvedic system of medicine however does not recognise the above method of digestion. But the ancient seers recognised comprehensive and complicated methods of digestion which is unknown to other systems of medicine. It is scientific and to be adopted by the physician who wants to treat diseases according to the Ayurvedic system of medicine. Ayurveda recognises the process of digestion involving 13 types of agnis, namely, jatharagni which is the most important Agni, seven dhatvagnis and five bhuta agnis. Jatharagni is an important agni contained in pachaka pitta and is the root of all the agnis of the body. Ayurveda believes that most of the diseases of the body are due to the deficiency or aggravation of the jatharagni. Its deficiency causes anorexia (loss of appetite) and dyspepsia, vomiting and diarrhoea. The following are the six important factors which aid in the process of digestion: pachaka pitta, samana vayu, moisture, kledaka kapha, time and a proper combination of the first five. Samana vayu which propels the food into the stomach from the mouth and brings it near the jatharagni, aids in digestion, assimilation and in differentiating between vital food essence and excreta. The vital food essence called rasa gets absorbed in the body,

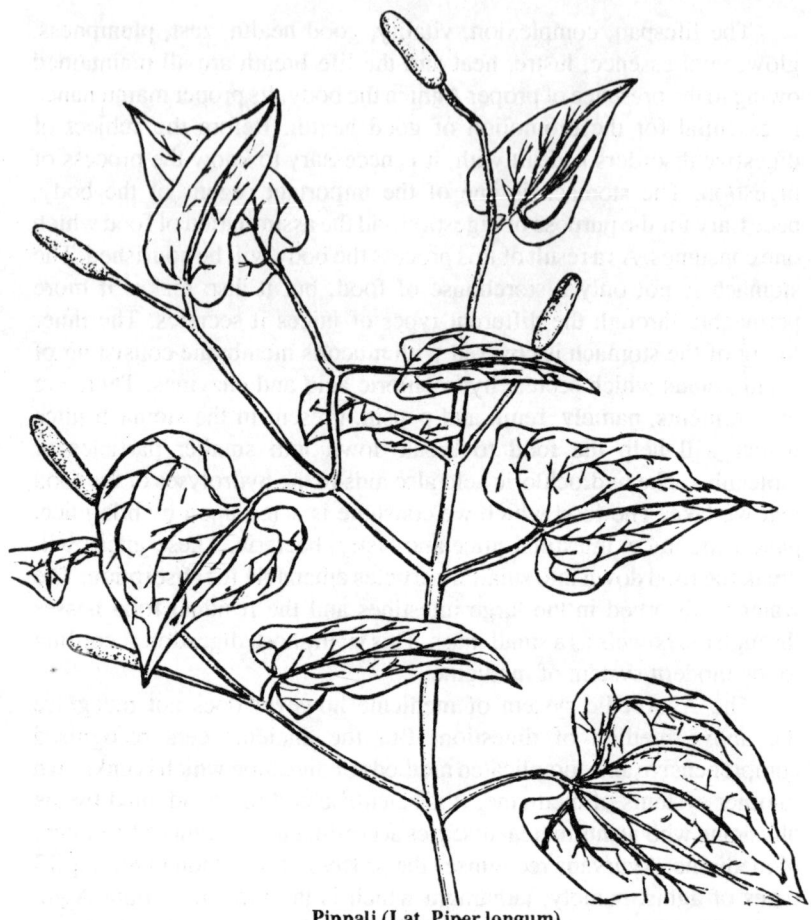

Pippali (Lat. Piper longum)

which it nourishes. The excretas like urine, faeces, sweat, etc, are
expelled out of the body. The kledaka kapha which helps in moistening
the food that we take at fixed time are necessary for softening the food
and for completing the necessary process of digestion. Hereafter the
diseases and disorders of digestion will be dealt with.

ANOREXIA

Causes and Symptoms: Anorexia is nothing but a loss of appetite for
food. This may be due to physical causes or due to mental causes like

an hysterical aversion to food. In this disease the patient will not have a taste for food.

Ayurveda has dealt with it as an independent disease and classified it into five varieties.

(1) *Vataja Anorexia:* In this case astringent taste in the mouth and pain in the area of upper part of the stomach are found; (2) *Pittaja Anorexia:* In this case symptoms of distaste and putrified taste in mouth are found; (3) *Kaphaja Anorexia:* In this case saltish and sweet taste in mouth associated with viscidness and bad taste and odour with salivation are found; (4) *Agantuja Anorexia:* In this case taste and uneasiness are found.

Treatment: The treatment lies in eradicating or removing the root cause of anorexia. The patient must be given a medicine which is an appetiser and carminative. The following prescriptions can be taken with resounding benefit:

Fresh green ginger with rock salt should be taken in a dose of five grains each, twice daily before meals; or ginger juice with honey (one teaspoonful with one-fourth teaspoonful of honey) should be given twice daily before meals for seven days.

The following tablets can also be taken either alone or together: Rochaka gutika, Drakshadi gutika and Kshudhakari Vati etc., 1 to 2 tablets twice a day before meals.

CONSTIPATION

Causes and Symptoms: Most people suffer from constipation due to sedentary habit and taking excessive food frequently. The patient wants to pass stools but he cannot do so. Constipation leads to heaviness, headache, loss of appetite and no interest in doing any work. When food is present in the intestine for a longer period, naturally it will lead to putrefaction and flatulence. Sometimes acute constipation may lead to distension of the stomach with severe pain in the abdomen.

Treatment: The patient must regularise his food habits and he must take food at regular and fixed intervals. He must avoid irritant, spicy, fatty food and too refined cereals and rice. It is better for the patient to eat light meals along with a little quantity of milk, fruit juices and boiled vegetables and leafy vegetables. Hot water must be taken frequently if he feels thirsty. If the child is suffering from constipation then a suppository prepared with stock of betel leaf coated with castor oil must be introduced into the rectum. Hot poultice of Eranda leaves or Kidmari leaves can also be applied to the abdomen of the child. The following remedies are used daily by Indian villagers: The powder of liquorice root is to be given along with jaggery and water for a period of one week. Dose: one tola powder with ¼ tola of jaggery. In case of old constipation, senna leaves 4 parts and ripe pods of cassias fistula 3 parts, chebulic myrobalan 5 parts, are to be powdered and made into pills of 15 to 30grs., one pill should be taken twice daily by adults for a week to fifteen days. Madhu Yastyadi churna, Pancha Sakera churna and Sukha Virechana churna, anyone of the above powders should be taken in a dose of 30 to 40grs. twice daily after food along with hot water or milk. In case of chronic constipation Abhayarishta must be taken in a dose of half to one ounce with an equal quantity of boiled and cold water after meals for 15 days. Alternatively milk with castor oil (one glass of hot milk with 1 teaspoon of castor oil) should be taken after food at bed time for a fortnight. If the patient gets loose bowls then he should either stop or lessen the dosage.

The patient must be advised to walk in the fresh air for at least half an hour to one hour either in the morning or in the evening.

Flatulence: It is nothing but irritation of either the stomach or intestines due to the accumulation of either gas or flatus in the intestine or stomach. It is produced due to defective digestion. It is called Admana in Ayurveda. The gas must either be expelled through the mouth or through the anus, otherwise, it produces pain in the region of the heart and increases its rate (tachycardia). A patient who is ignorant of this disease will suspect it to be a heart disease.

Treatment: Food or drugs which are either carminative or gas reducing have to be administered to cure this disease.

1.   Ajamoda seeds two parts with 1 part of aniseed (saunf) must be given along with sugar in a dose of 10 to 20grs. at a time, twice daily. Alternatively the powder of ginger, black pepper, mint (pudina) and celery seeds (ajamoda) are to be taken in equal quantities and to be taken in a dose of 10 to 30grs. in the morning and evening for seven days. Any one of the following medicines can also be taken to remedy the flatulence:

1.   *Hingvashtaka Churna:* Hingvashtaka Churna or Panchacola Churna in a dose of 2 teaspoonful once a day must be taken on an empty stomach and Kumariasava can be taken in a dosage of one ounce with equal quantity of water after meals twice daily.

The patient must be advised not to take food which produces gas, like potatoes, pulses, beans and fatty foods, especially when his food is not properly digested daily.High carbohydrate, like rice, should be avoided. Buttermilk is advised along with old rice. The patient should be told to avoid hurry, worry, anxiety, and tension while eating meals.

DYSPEPSIA

Causes and Symptoms: It is nothing but indigestion. During the digestion of food, the patient experiences pain in the region of the stomach, flatulence, belching, foul taste in the mouth, discomfort and heart-burn. This is mainly due to the deficiency of digestive fire and enzymes of body. In these cases there will be a history of either overeating or eating at irregular intervals or taking unhealthy food. This is called Agnimandhya in Ayurveda which is produced due to the vitiation of three doshas (vata, pitta and kapha); it may be noted here that pain occurs due to aggravation of vata and pitta produces burning sensation and vitiation of kapha produces either nausea or vomiting or both.

Treatment: Prevention is better than cure is an adage. It holds good here also. We must educate the public to take proper food at the proper time in a proper quantity. Fresh and hot food must be taken in a good atmosphere. One should eat when the previous meal is digested and not eat in a hurry or with emotion, anger or tension. One should take food which should not be heavy and it must be properly masticated. Food and sleep are also responsible for producing vitiation of doshas, so they must be taken properly. A nourishing diet in accordance with proper seasons is required. Especially in winter, sour, unctuous and saline foods, meat of aquatic animals and birds must be taken. In summer one must take more liquid, sweets, juices, and drinks with their family and friends. Milk, rice, and meat of animals which dwell in the forest must be consumed. Alcohol needs to be avoided, or only consumed after mixing it with a large quantity of water. In winter, however, he is permitted wine with meat soup or meat preparations.

One should take rock salt with ginger 20grs.twice daily after meals. Hingvashtaka Churna is a specific remedy according to Ayurveda for dyspepsia and it consists of Hing (asafoetida), Shunthi (Zingiber officinale), Pippali (Piper longum), Maricha (piper nigrum), Ajamoda (corum roxburghianum), Jiraka (cuminnum cyminum) and black cummin seed.

Another specific remedy is buttermilk which has an astringent and sour taste, is easily digestible and also acts as a digestive stimulant. It wards off both kapha and vata or gas in the body. The following are other known remedies:

1. Chitraka powder 2gms.
2. Jiraka powder 2gms.
3. Maricha powder 2gms.
4. Mahashanka vati two tablets twice daily.
5. Haritaki churna.
6. Narayana churna each 2gms. with sugar must be given at bedtime along with pippalyasava and draksharishta each 1 teaspoonful.

Lavana Bhaskara Churna, Lashunadi vati 1 to 2 tablets after food may be given to the patient.

Any one of the above prescriptions must be taken.

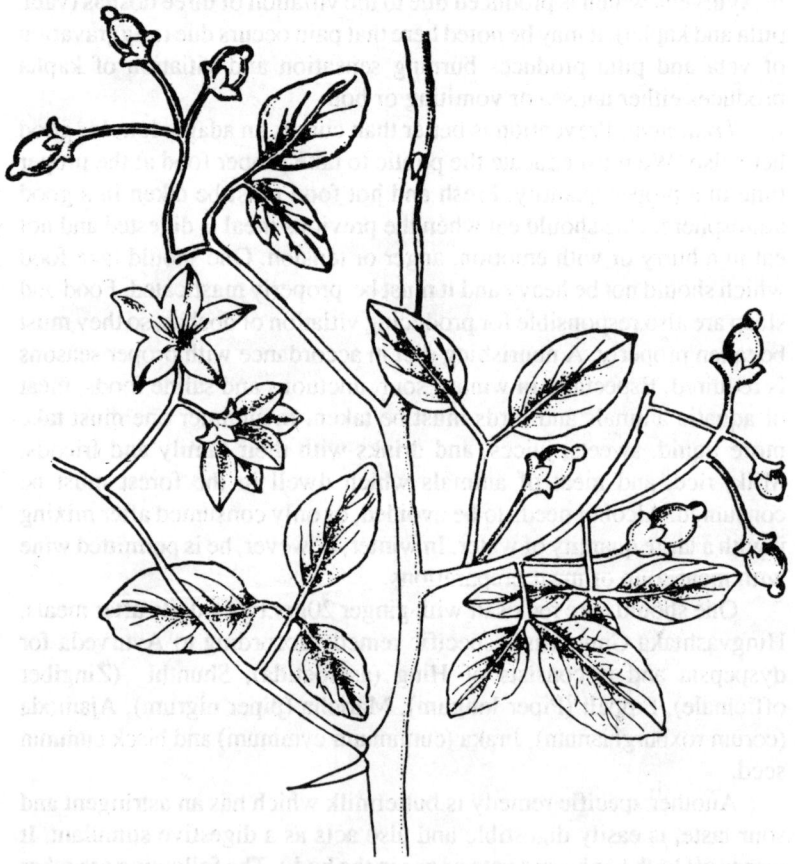

Bilva (Lat. Eagles Marmele Scorr)

DIARRHOEA

It is condition where stools are passed loosely through the anus. These stools may contain water, formed or unformed or solid digested or undigested food in small or large quantity. This is due to defective digestive fire which is incapable of digesting food that is fatty or heavy, or mixed with poisonous materials or containing virulent bacteria like typhoid, fever, cholera, or intestinal tuberculosis, the diseases of the heart, lungs, kidney, liver and stomach. According to Ayurveda, diarrhoea is caused by the vitiation of (1) vata, (2) pitta, (3) kapha, (4) vitiation of all the three, (5) due to sudden fright, shock of death of a loved one, (6) Amatisara, it is caused by amadosha or undigested food.

INFANTILE DIARRHOEA

Causes and Symptoms: Children who get diarrhoea have either drunk defective or infected milk or caught an infection in the intestinal tract. If a child is taking mother's milk, any digestive disorder of the mother may produce diarrhoea in the child which will be associated with vomiting and a griping pain in the stomach. The stools of the sick child will be either liquid or semi-liquid, with a foul small and a yellowish or greenish tinge. It may be noted here that children do get diarrhoea at the time of teething and the child will cry day and night. He may bite the nipples of his mother. If the condition is neglected it will lead to dehydration and eventually the emaciation and death of the child.

Treatment: A paste prepared from the inner bark of the mango tree must be applied on the child's abdomen. Or *dadima* flowers ¼ tola, Shalmasli leaves ¼ tola, Soumph ¼ tola fried in pure ghee must be taken in the dose of ¼ tola and burnt ashes of Papaversomniferum ¼ tola and all these should be mixed and pounded and tablets of the dose of 1 gunja should be made. It should be given with breast milk 3 times daily in order to stop loose motions in children. Balachaturbhadra churna must be given in a dose of 4 grains. It is a known remedy for the above complaint. Goroc nadi vatika can also be given in a dose of 1 grain 3 times daily. If the patient suffers from loose stools with vomiting, 1½ grains of powdered seed of nutmeg *(Jaiphal)* can be given in order to stop the gripping pain in the stomach.

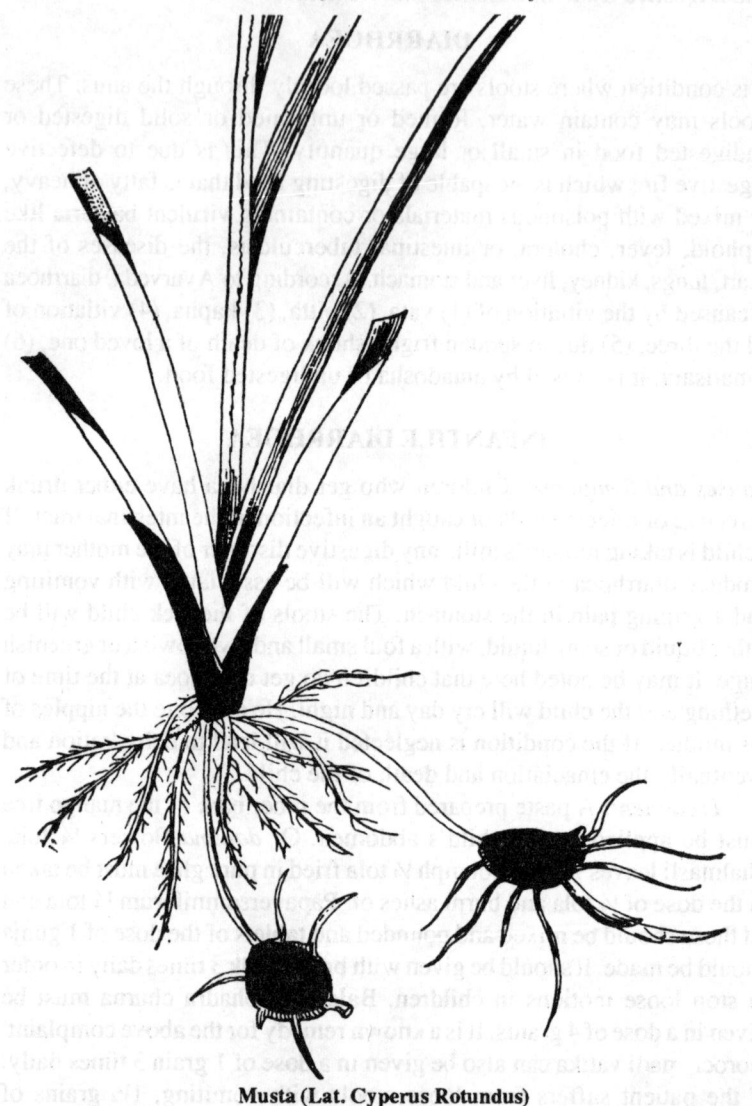

Musta (Lat. Cyperus Rotundus)

Gripe water which is sold in the market contains harmful drugs even though they are stated as carminatives, if they are continued for an indefinite period. Ayurveda advocates a very famous medicine called *Musta* (Cyperus rotundus) for curing infantile diarrhoea. Its root should be given in a dose of 1 to 2 grs. along with honey 2 to 3 times a day. It can also be given in the form of Mustarista, i.e. by boiling 3 grains of musta in milk twice daily. It may be noted here that the milk of the mother will

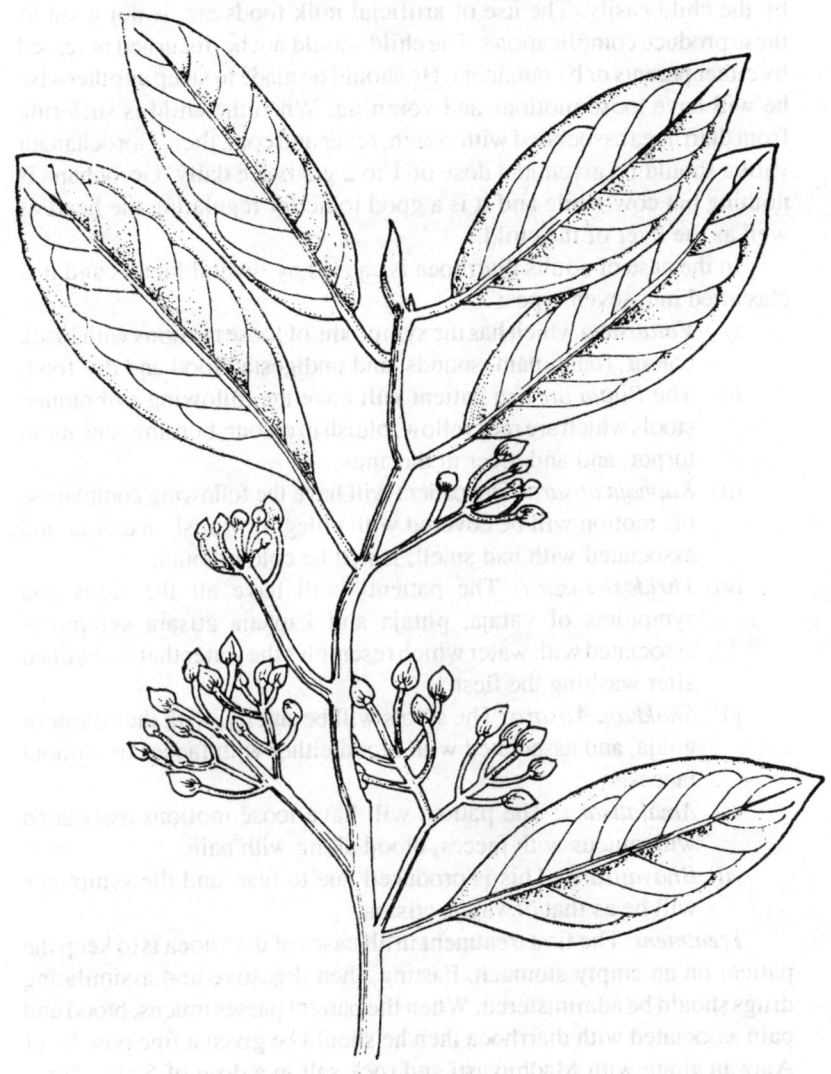

Jathiphala (Lat. Myristica Frograns)

be vitiated by vata, pitta and kapha so the mother who breast-feeds the child should be given proper treatment to correct any such defects. *No milk is equal to breast milk.* Since cow's milk contains less fat than buffalo's milk, it is the best substitute for breast milk as it can be digested by the child easily. The use of artificial milk foods etc. is not good as these produce complications. The child should not be disturbed or teased by either parents or by outsiders. He should be made to sleep as otherwise he will have loose motions and vomiting. When the child is suffering from diarrhoea associated with cough, fever and cold, then, Gorochanadi vatika should be given in a dose of 1 to 2 grs.twice daily. Gorochana is nothing but cow's bile and it is a good tonic for regulating the heart as well as the liver of the child.

In the case of adults diarrhoea is caused by several factors and it is classified into seven types:

   i)   *Vatatisara* which has the symptoms of loose motions with black colour, foam, pain, sounds, and undigested food and dry food.

   ii) The *Pitaja atisara* patient will have the following symptoms: stools which are red, yellow, bluish in colour, burning sensation, torpor, and and ulcer in the anus.

   iii) *Kaphaja atisara.* The patient will have the following complaints: the motion will be covered with phlegm, whitish in colour and associated with bad smell; it will be cold to touch.

   iv) *Thridoshatisara:* The patient will have all the signs and symptoms of vataja, pittaja and kaphaja atisara symptoms associated with water which resembles the water that is obtained after washing the flesh.

   v)   *Shokhaja Atisara:* The stools will be smelly, with the colour of gunja, and associated with blood either with faeces or without faeces.

   vi) *Amajatisara:* The patient will have loose motions associated with mucus with faeces, blood along with pain.

   vii) *Bhayatisara:* This is produced due to fear and the symptoms will be as that of vataja atisara.

Treatment: The first treatment in all cases of diarrhoea is to keep the patient on an empty stomach. Fasting, then digestive and assimilating drugs should be administered. When the patient passes mucus, blood and pain associated with diarrhoea then he should be given a fine powder of Ajawan along with Madhuyasti and rock salt in a dose of 5 grs., 2grs., 2grs. respectively along with butter 3 times a day. The powder of Abhaya in a dose of 20 to 30grs. should be given every four hours along with hot water in the initial stages itself. The same powder can also be given with buttermilk. As soon as loose motions are controlled then coriander with dadima juice should be given twice a day for a week. The dried powder of the seeds of Bilva should be given along with dry ginger and jaggery with buttermilk in a dose of 5grs., 2grs., and 5grs. resepectively twice daily for a period of one week. Generally the following drugs can be given: Kutaja churna, Dadimastaka churna (each ¼ tola) twice daily with buttermilk. If there is pain Shankhabhasma can be added to it in a dose of 200mg. twice in a day.

Tablets: 1. Shankha Vati 2 tablets twice daily 2. Kutajaghanavati 2 tablets twice daily.

Diet and Regimen: In the initial stages it is advised to keep the patient fasting or on a light diet like ganji, the liquid prepared from fried rice along with coriander and dry ginger which should be taken, each about ¼ tola. This gruel is prepared and given to the patient twice daily. In case of diarrhoea old rice with buttermilk, young and fresh brinjal etc., may be given to the patient. Only hot water should be given to the patient to drink. The patient must be asked not to take salt, pepper, Masha, jaggery, wheat, garlic, tender coconut water, sugarcane juice, indigestible food and to avoid coitus, abhyanga (anointing of the body), excessive walking, awakening at night and smoking.

DYSENTERY

Symptoms. Dysentery is a condition wherein the patient will notice passing of blood in his stools along with mucus or with faeces or without faeces. It is due to the inflammation of the lower part of the large intestine. The patient will experience pain in the abdomen with the other symptoms already explained. Modern medicine has classified dysentery into two major types according to their infective organisms: (a) Amoebic Dysentery, and (b) Bacillary Dysentery.

In amoebic dysentery there will be mucus present in the stools along with Bacteria Entamoeba Hystalytica and in case of bacillary desentery there will be more blood in the stools with Shegella group of organisms. In amoebic dysentery the frequency of passing stools is less when compared to bacillary dysentery. In Ayurveda amoebic dysentery is called Pravahika and bacillary dysentery is known as Raktatisara. The line of treatment given for diarrhoea holds good for dysentery also. Pravahika is nothing but a condition wherein the patient will pass stools with great exertion at the time of defaecation. The patient will pass stools very frequently with tenesmus and pain. The quantity of stools will be less but there will be plenty of mucus and blood.

Treatment: In dysentery with mucus the seeds of Henna Plant (Mehandi) are effective. The seed should be powdered and mixed with ghee and should be taken (one ball the size of a betelnut) twice or thrice daily. Bael fruit should be taken with jaggery in a dose of five to 20grs. thrice a day along with buttermilk. Sometimes dry ginger with bael fruit and buttermilk works wonders.

CHOLERA

Causes and Symptoms: Cholera is a condition characterised by vomiting, diarrhoea and severe pain in the abdomen. It is caused by Vibriocholerae (Comma Bacillus). It is found in the faeces of the persons suffering from cholera. It is spread through five ways, namely (1) Flies, (2) Fomites, (3) Faeces, (4) Water, and (5) Vegetables.

In the initial stages (3 to 12 hours) the patient will experience painless diarrhoea and vomiting. This will be followed by severe cramps in the stomach, intestine and restlessness associated with severe thirst. In the later stage of the disease the patient will develop fever and his body will be warm even at the stage of his death.

In Ayurveda this is called Vishoochika and it is one of the most severe diseases of the stomach and intestines. In cases where the signs and symptoms are only vomiting and diarrhoea with fever in the later stage of the disease, cholera is produced due to Ama.

Treatment: Ayurveda advocates the physician not to stop the diarrhoea and vomiting at least for a few hours till all the toxins are expelled from the body. But the only complication which is severe in nature is dehydration due to the loss of fluid from the body. It can be prevented by the administration of liquid extract of Ajwain (Arka), mixed with a sufficient quantity of coriander water. It should be given in small doses. Karpurdiarka can also be given. Ajwain should be taken in a dose of one tola added to one litre of water and reduced to ¼ litre and about 10 grains of Pacchakarpura (Camphor) must be added to it; it should be sufficiently stirred after keeping it in a sterile bottle. The patient should be given a little quantity of this mixture now and then till vomiting and diarrhoea are stopped. In order to prevent vomiting Mayurapicha bhasma should be given with honey. It is also well known in India that in order to stop cholera juice extracted from the fresh leaves of Thuvarkkadal should be filtered and given to the patient in small doses. Cholera can also be sucessfully treated by administering the juice of onion and bittergourd. One spoonful every half an hour should be given till the symptoms subside. Tablets of the size of small pepper should be prepared by taking the following drugs, and grinding them in a mortar with a pestle continuously for more than three hours. Administer one tablet per hour till the condition is cured. The drugs to be pounded are opium, jathipal, lavanga, kumkum keshari and karpur. Digestive stimulants are advocated in Vishoochika.

The following prepartions can also be used to cure the disease:
1. Sanjivani vati 1-2 tablets per day.
2. Vishuchika vati 1-2 tablets per day.
3. Visuchidhavamsan rasa 200mg.-400mg. per day.
4. Arka vati 1-2 tablets per day.
5. Mritsanjivani sura 5 to 10 drops and Lasunadi vati 1-2 tablets per day.

Any one of the above prescriptions should be given alone, in a proper dose. Mritsanjivani sura is the best medicine for curing this disease.

Diet. A patient suffering from cholera should be kept on a liquid diet. No solid foods should be given as it is not going to be digested by the patient. Gruel prepared from fried and broken rice are to be given to the patient. He should be allowed to drink only hot water which has been cooled.

SPRUE SYNDROME

Causes and Symptoms: It is a digestive disorder produced due to the lessening of the gastric juice and enzymes in the body. It is characterised by the passage of loose and fatty stools associated with anemia, loss of weight, sore tongue and in later stages, emaciation. According to modern medicine it is a defect in the metabolism, as a result of which fat will not be absorbed from the intestines. Later on, the carbohydrates, minerals and vitamins are not going to be absorbed either.

In Ayurveda this ailment is called Sangrahani (Grahani roga). It is so called because the grahana shakti or grasping power or contracting power of the intestine will be lost. Hence, there will be no proper absorption of food, so the patient has loose and frothy stools associated with pain in the abdomen. It is due to the defect in the pittadharakala (mucous membrane) of the lower part of the stomach and upper part of the small intestine. It is the seat of jatharagni.

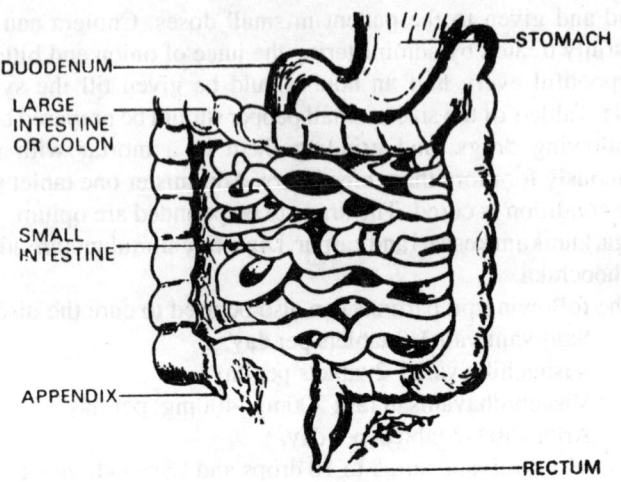

Small Intestine

Treatment: The best treatment is to activate the agni by means of digestive and assimilating drugs. Example: Chitrak (Plumbago Zeylanicum) should be administered in a dose of twenty to forty grains along with buttermilk which is mixed with long pepper, honey and burnt ashes of unripe bael pulp. Guduchi (Tinosphora cordifolia wild), Mustaka (Tubercle of nut grass) and Ativsha (root atis), are to be taken in equal quantities. A decoction is prepared by adding sufficient quantity of water and reducing it to one-fourth its quantity. The following prepared yogas can also be given to cure the disease: *Rasaparpati,* is the drug of choice in treating the sprue syndrome. However, Panchamrita Parpati (200mg.twice daily), Babbularishta (½ to 1 ounce) Mustakarista (½ to 1 ounce), Grahani Kapata rasa (200mg. per day) can be givien. *Jathipaladi* churna should be given in a dose of one tola twice daily; dugdha vati can also be given in a dose of 1 to 2 tablets twice daily with buttermilk. Arista is given in the dose of one ounce twice daily with an equal quantity of water.

Massage: Grahani Mihira Taila is to be applied on the abdomen of the patient who is suffering from sprue syndrome, chronic diarrhoea and dysentery as it tones up the bowels.

THIRST

Signs and Symptoms: Thirst is a desire for water. It occurs whenever there is a great demand for water in the body. It is a disease condition in which the patient has dryness in the throat. It is produced due to many causes. According to the Ayurvedic system of medicine either excess of pitta or loss of somaguna of the body tissues will produce a condition called thirst. It is clinically classified into seven types. They are: vataja, pittaja, kaphaja, kshataja, amaja and bhaktaja.

Vataja Thirst

The patient will complain of *throbbing* pain in the temporal region with giddiness and distaste in the mouth.

Pittaja Thirst

The patient feels bitterness in the mouth and there will be a burning sensation in the body.

Kaphaja Thirst

(1) Saltish and sweetish taste in the mouth, (2) Anorexia and (3) Nausea.

Kshataja Thirst: It is produced due to injury. Kshataja thirst is produced due to diseases such as tuberculosis or any other chronic disease.

Amaja Thirst : Amaja thirst is produced due to the indigestion of food.

Bhaktaja Thirst: This is produced due to the intake of food.

Treatment: A patient suffering from thirst should be given fried Mudga seeds and fried rice. These must be taken in equal quantity and a decoction prepared. To the cold decoction of one ounce, add one teaspoonful of honey with ¼ teaspoonful of sugar and give it to the patient. The ashes of dry grapes and big cardamom should be burnt along with the outer cover of the coconut shell. It should be given in a dose of 20grs. to 40grs. with honey. Heated brick which is already cleaned must be dipped in cow's curd, filtered and given to the patient for drinking. The patient can also be given buttermilk with a little quantity of sugar, honey and ghee in different proportions along with ¼ tola each of pepper and cardamom. Even giving honey frequently along with cold water will stop the thirst. A decoction which is prepared with turmeric should be given with sugar and honey. The following preparations are also effective if they are taken in a suitable dose. Shadanga Paniya one teaspoonful 3 to 4 times daily. Rasadivati 1 tablet thrice daily. Laja Manda 1 teaspoonful twice daily, Ushirasava, Chandansasava can be taken in a dose of 1 teaspoonful thrice daily.

Diet: Old rice or gruel, buttermilk, coriander, *Hingu* (Hingu), onion, grapes and green gram.

Smoking, exercise, fomentation or any other activities which increase pitta in the body, and salt are strictly prohibited.

VOMITING

Signs and Symptoms: It is nothing but ejecting out the contents of the stomach through the mouth. In modern medicine it is called emeses. This is produced due to many causes but here the major causes will be explained: mental worries, intestinal worms, pregnancy in females and indigestion if the food is not adjustable to an individual's body. In Ayurveda, clinically chhardi has been classified under the five headings: (1) Vataja, (2) Pittaja, (3) Kaphaja, (4) Tridoshaja, and (5) Dvishtartha Samyogata.

Vataja type of vomiting is characterised by dryness of the mouth, an astringent taste in the mouth and pain in the chest. In *pittaja* type of vomiting there will be sour eructations, a burning sensation and a sour taste in the mouth. The patient may vomit bile which will be yellow in colour associated with dryness of the mouth, giddiness and thirst. In the *kaphaja* type of vomiting there will be a lot of white mucus associated with slimy secretion and a salty taste in the mouth. In *tridoshaja* type of vomiting the symptoms and signs of the above three doshas will be noticed. In Dvishtartha Samyogata vomiting is produced due to food poisoning and also putrified and abnoxious smell, etc.

Treatment: Firstly, it is better to avoid the causative factors which produce the vomiting. Secondly, the patient should not consume food or drinks which induce vomiting. The burnt ash of peacock feather (Mayura Pichha Bhasmas) should be given in a dose of 3 to 4grs. along with honey 3-4 times in a day. Another famous remedy for stopping vomiting is to give the juice of unripe kapittha along with honey. The burnt ash of the husk of cardamom is also a very good remedy to relieve this condition. Bilvadi (Acgle Marmelos Corr) lehya along with the juice of coriander is also effective in these cases. Coconut water can be given in combination with honey and pepper.

The following prepared medicines can also be given:

a.   Eladivati (Elettaria Cardamomum) 1-2 tablets per day, Chardiripu 1-2 tablets per day.

b.   Rasadi Churna 30 to 40grs. twice daily.

c.   Lajamanda 2-4 teaspoonful twice or thrice in a day.

ULCERS OF THE STOMACH

Causes: Ulcers are a discontinuity of the skin or the mucous membrane or any other organs of the body, or any break in the tissues which is not going to be healed quickly. Modern medicine states that there are several causes which produce ulcers in the stomach, but Ayurveda has dealt with shula (pain) and states that it is caused due to stress and strain, hurry and worry. These are the important causes for the production of stomach ulcers. Ayurveda clinically classified udarashula (abdominal pain) into eight categories: (1) Vataja, (2) Pittaja, (3) Kaphaja, (4) Vatapittaja, (5) Vata Kaphaja, (6) Pitta Kaphaja, (7) Tridoshaja and (8) Ama-pradoshaja shoola.

In addition to the above classification of shoolas, parinama shoola, Annadrava-shoola, Vit-shoola, Hrid-shoola, etc. are also found in Ayurvedic literature.

COLIC PAIN

It is called vataja shoola in Ayurveda and is produced due to the retention of flatus, gas and faeces in the bowels as a result of which there is

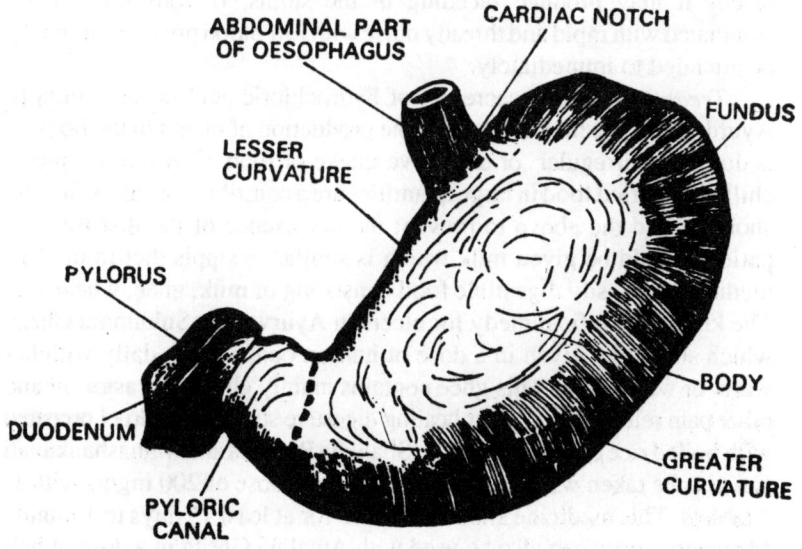

Stomach

distension and pain. This pain may be either in an increasing pattern or decreasing pattern. It may subside with the administration of oily foods and massage. It will be increased on emptying the bowels. It is nothing but a periodical spasm in the abdominal organ. The decoction of root of castor oil plant prepared with ginger, fried asafoetida and rock salt should be administered in a dose of one ounce twice daily.

Pittaja-Shoola: Thirst, burning sensation, desire for cold things and an acute pain in the abdomen. Dathri Louha should be given in a dose of 12grs. with honey or ghee.

Kaphaja Shoola: Nausea, depression and anorexia and abdominal pain on taking food, associated with constipation and headache. Shoola Varjini Vati 1-2 pills (10grs. each) should be given twice daily with warm water.

Duodenal ulcer is produced in the area of the duodenum. It is stated in Ayurveda that grahani is the seat of pitta or jathatagni which is necessary for proper digestion of food in the body. The duodenal ulcer is called parinama shoola in Ayurveda. In the duodenum, pancreatic juice, bile juice and stomach juice act on the food which is to be digested. So grahani plays an important role in producing defective or incomplete absorption of food and can lead to a lot of complications. If the ulcer bleeds it may produce bleeding in the stools. If vomiting occurs, associated with rapid and thready pulse with low blood pressure, it should be attended to immediately.

Treatment: Hyper secretion of hydrochloric acid or amla pitta in Ayurdveda is the major cause for the production of ulcers in the body. It is due to the irregular or excessive intake of food. Consuming spices, chillies and fried food in large quantities are a contributing cause. So, one should avoid the above to prevent the occurrence of the disease. The patient should be given milk which is similar to sippis diet in modern medicine, or easily digestible food consisting of milk, ghee, wheat, etc. The known specific remedy for ulcers in Ayurveda is Sukumara Ghrita which should be given in a dose of half an ounce twice daily with hot water or warm milk. This ghee contains mainly ghee and castor oil and other pain relieving and ulcer healing digestive stimulants. Gruel prepared with boiled rice can also be given. Shankha Bhasma and Mahashankavati can also be taken with ghee or hot water in a dose of 200 mgms with 1-2 tablets. This medicine should be taken for at least 15 days to 1 month, Shatavari Ghrita can also be used with Amalaki Ghrita in a dose of half teaspoonful twice daily. Even taking only Amalaki powder (Emblica officinalis) of 1 teaspoonful four times daily has been found to be beneficial in ulcer patients. The patient should avoid mental stress, irregular intake of food, constipation, spicy, irritant foods and foods which produce vata in the body.

HYPOCHLORHYDRIA

Signs and Symptoms: Pain will start as soon as the food is eaten or at the time of digestion. The pain will persist till the bile is vomited from the stomach. The causative factors are the same as that of the duodenal ulcer. It is called Annadrava shoola in Ayurveda.

Treatment: The powder of Amalaki (Embelic myrobalan) in a dose of 30grs. should be given thrice daily with honey. Lavanamla should be administered after getting it diluted with water in a dose of 10 to 15 drops, per time 2 to 3 times daily.

HAEMATEMESIS

Causes: The causative factors are the same as that of gastric ulcer, duodenal ulcer, gastric cancer and chronic gastritis.

Symptoms: Vomiting of blood from the stomach is called haematemesis. It is always mixed with food particles and mucus or water. It should not be confused with bleeding in the mouth. It is called Urdhwaga Rakta pitta and specially termed as Rakta vami.

Treatment: All cooling measures should be adopted. The juice of Kusmanda (Benincasa Hispida) in a dose of one ounce twice daily should be given along with 30grs. of Amalaki (Emblica officinalis) or Pravala Pisti should be given along with Laksha in a dose of 30grs. each twice daily with honey or ice water.

Diet: Old rice, Dadima, Amalaka, Patola (Trochosanthes Dioica) and mung dal, banana, ghee, butter and milk are useful. Irritant spicy and hot foods are strictly forbidden. The patient is advised bed rest with physical and mental rest.

COLIC PAIN

Stomach ache: This is produced due to the causes which may produce indigestion and duodenal and stomach disorders. It is called Amayshaya shoola in Ayurveda.

Treatment: Half an ounce of ginger juice with 2 teaspoonful of castor oil will relieve the pain.

Fomentation: Leaves of paris (Thespeasia populenea) pasted with hot castor oil should be applied on the abdomen.

Naryana churna in a dose of 30grs. with water or Ajeernari rasa (1 to 2 tablets) are very effective in curing stomach pain.

BILIARY COLIC

It is nothing but a pain which is observed in the liver area. It is due to the spasm of the muscles of the bile duct or due to the obstruction of bile stones in the bile duct.

Treatment: Narasaradi Puspa should be given in a dose of 10grs. with water twice daily. Amritarista in a dose of 2 teaspoons with 10 grs. of ashes of Talamakhana (Steracantha longolia) should be given for a week.

INTESTINAL WORMS

Causes: An individual who is in the habit of taking excess sweets, curds, fluids, starch food and jaggery without doing any exercise, sleeping at day time and eating unwholesome food is likely to get intestinal worms. In Ayurveda the krimis (worms and bacterias) are of four types.

1. Purishaja, 2. Shlesmaja, 3. Shonitaja, and 4. Malaja.

According to their origin they are classified into 20 types. Out of these twenty the Bahya krimis are produced outside the body due to the insanitary condition of either skin or hair, or the wearing of dirty clothes.

Shlesmaja or Kapahaja Krimis: Vomiting, constipation, indigestion, anorexia, nausea, salivation, sneezing, bodyache, rashes on the skin, headache, cough and cold, etc.

Purishaja Krimis: Itching sensation in the anus, throbbing pain, horripilation, roughness of the skin, diarrhoea, weakness, anorexia, watering from the mouth, pain in the cardiac orifice, passing of the worms in the stools and pallor due to anaemia.

Treatment: The patient must keep himself clean and should avoid the factors which are explained in the causative factors for the worms. Next, the medicine should be administered to remove the worms from the body. There are two types: Krimihara, and Krimipatana. They are called 'anthelmentic'. For expelling intestinal worms, Vidanga (Embelia ribes) is a known specific remedy. It should be given in a dosage of one-fourth tola (1 teaspoonful) with curd, 2 teaspoonful early in the morning on an empty stomach. It expels both round worms and tapeworms. It should be given for 10 days. It should be associated with a mild purgative. Kampilla is the powder obtained from fruits of Mellotus Philippinensis. It should be given (2 to 3grs.) for children with honey for 3 days. The following prepared drugs can also be given. Krimighna vati 1 to 2 tablets twice daily or Krimi Kuthara rasa 1-2 tablets twice daily or Vidangarista 1 ounce (adults) twice daily after meals. It is a good appetiser, cures indigestion and expels worms from the intestine.

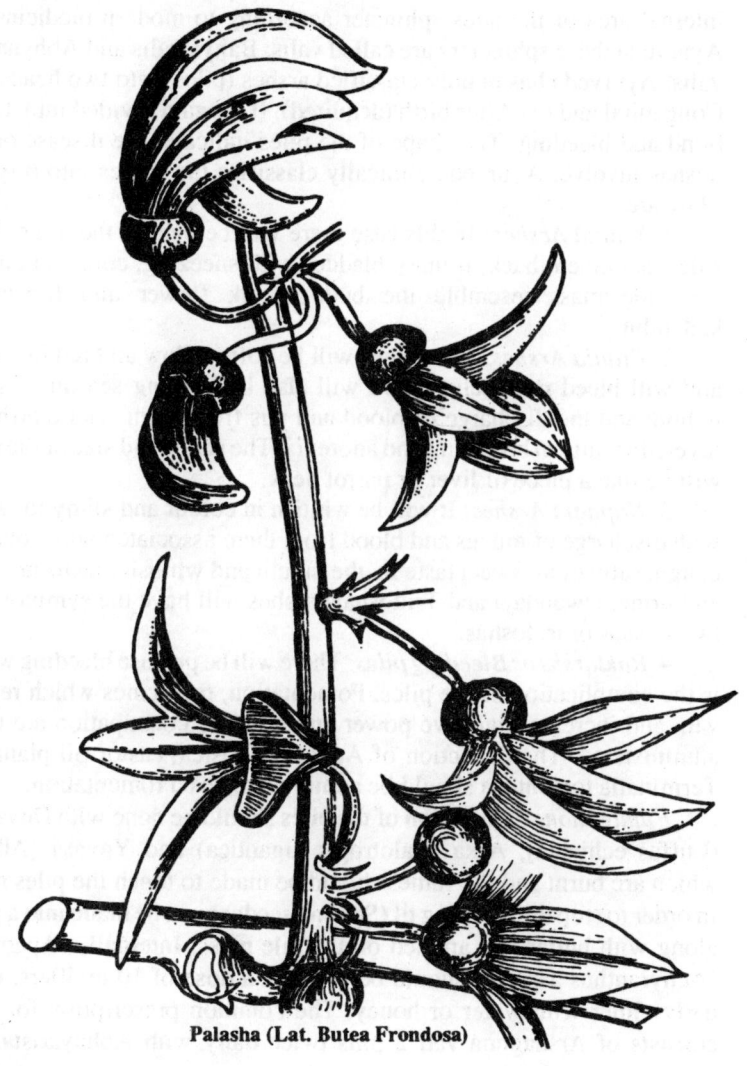

Palasha (Lat. Butea Frondosa)

PILES

Causes: Irregular intake of food, hard foods, dry foods, irritant foods like chillies or riding on a vehicle continuously for a long time will produce piles or arshes. This is according to the Ayurvedic system of medicine. The condition is produced due to the varicosity of the veins around the anus. It may be either in the external area of sphincter of the anus or the internal area of the anus sphincter according to modern medicine. In Ayurveda these sphincters are called valis: Bahya valis and Abhyantara valis. Ayurveda has mainly classified arshes (piles) into two heads: (1) Congenital and (2) After birth (acquired). It is again divided into dry or blind and bleeding. The shape of the piles indicates the disease or the doshas involve. Ayurveda clinically classifies the arshes into 6 types. They are:

1. *Vataja Arshes:* In this case there will be pain in the thigh, loin, sides, abdomen, back, urinary bladder with sneezing, cold and cough. The pile mass resemble the buds of tik flower and flower of kadambh.

2. *Pittaja Arshes:* The arshes will be soft, yellow and red in colour and will bleed profusely. There will also be burning sensation, pain, itching and the discharge of blood and pus from them with diarrhoea, fever, diffculty in breathing and anorexia. The shape and size of the piles will be like a piece of liver or parrot beak.

3. *Kaphaja Arshes:* It will be whitish in colour and slimy to touch with discharge of mucus and blood from them associated with cold and cough, salivation, sweet taste in the mouth and whitish mucus in stools and urine. Dwandaja and Tridoshaja arshes will have the symptoms of two doshas or tridoshas.

4. *Raktarshs or Bleeding piles:* There will be profuse bleeding which is the complication of the piles. Fomentation, medicines which reduce vata and increase digestive power and regulate constipation are to be administered. The decoction of Adhotoda vasica, castor oil plant and Terminalia tomentosa should be administered as a fomentation.

Fumigation: Fumigation of the piles should be done with Devadali, (Luffas echinata), Arka (Calotropis gigantica) and Yavasa (Alhagi) which are burnt and the fumes should be made to touch the piles mass. In order to stop the bleeding til (Sesame seeds) must be made into a paste along with butter and applied on the pile mass. Internally, Apamarga (Achyranthus asperas) should be given in a dose of 10 to 30grs. twice daily either with water or honey. The common prescription for piles consists of Arshaghna vati 2 pills twice daily with Abhayarista, one ounce after meal. Swadista Virechana churna is a laxative. It must be administered 1 teaspoonful at bedtime with hot water.

The following prepared medicines can also be used: Arshonyt tablets (Charaka) or Pilex tablets (Himalaya) in a dose of 2 tablets twice daily: Externally Pilex or Arshonyt ointment must also be used. Whenever their is bleeding piles the Posex tablets are used in a dose of 2 tablets twice daily with Kutajarista one ounce twice daily.

3

THE RESPIRATORY SYSTEM
Diseases and Remedies

In this chapter the diseases of organs involved in respiration will be explained. In the chest cavity the main organs are trachea, bronchi, two

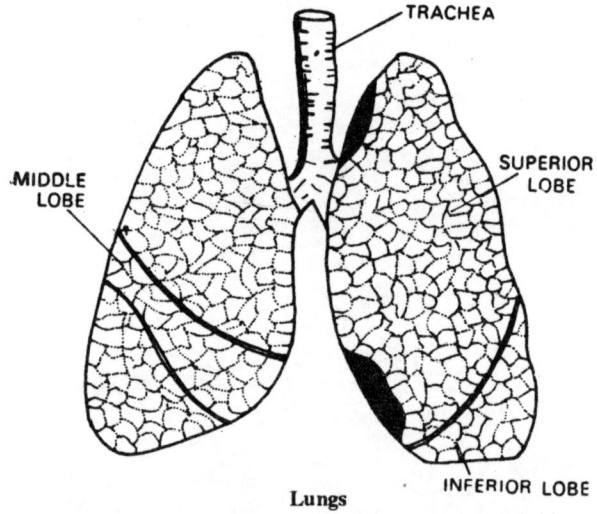

Lungs

lungs, the heart and the diaphragm. Respiration consists of inspiration and expiration. It is nothing but a process by which a man inhales pure air which is oxygenated and goes into the lungs and then exhales the impure air consisting of carbon dioxide. The important respiratory organs which are involved in the process of respiration are the nose, pharynx or the throat, the trachea or otherwise called the windpipe, the bronchi and the lungs.

Diseases of the Nose: The nose is also used to smell things but the inner lining of the nose is concerned with the production of many diseases. In Ayurveda the number of diseases of the nose is 34, out of which about a dozen of them are mainly due to inflammation and the rest are due to either boils or tumours which may produce foul smell in the phlegm. The very common condition thatt occurs in the nose is the common cold. In Ayurveda it is called Pratishyaya and it is called Coryza of the nose wherein the person who lives in a cold climate will have this catarrh. There is proverb that with medicine the cold with take 15 days to one month to cure but without medicine it will be aborted within a week. In Ayurveda it is not so but the cold can be controlled within one or two days with Ayurvedic medicine.

COMMON COLD

Causes: Exposing onself to cold, drinking cold water, etc., will produce pratishyaya. Generally all persons will not get it but if the resistance of the patient is less then he will catch a cold easily.

Symptoms: According to Ayurveda a cold is of 5 types:

1. Due to the aggravation of vata.
2. Due to aggravation of pitta.
3. Due to vitiation of kapha.
4. Due to the disorders of blood.
5. Due to the vitiation of the above 3 doshas.

The patient will have a running nose.

Treatment: A common home remedy is to inhale the fumes of burning turmeric powder(Curcuma longa). Another remedy is to take an equal quantity of dry grapes about two tolas, pepper two tolas and Madhu Yasti two tolas and powder them; make a tablet the size of bengal gram out of this mixture. This table should be administered twice daily along with hot water. Take one cup of cow's warm milk and add pepper and sugar candy about five grains each and give this to the patient twice daily. The ripe leaves of Ark (Calotropis gigantica) should be burnt and the ash twice daily along with honey. The bark of Ark, and Bura-sakar must be taken in equal quantity along with half of its dose of Trikatu (ginger, pepper and long pepper) and this should be burnt in fire and the smoke inhaled. The prepared medicines as Mahalakshmi Vilas or Naradiya Lakshmi Vilas in a dose of 200 milligrams twice daily with Madhuyasti or even the decoction of Sudharsana Churna will cure the cold. Chronic colds can be cured with Agastya Haritaki Rasayana in the dose of one teaspoon twice daily with milk or honey.

Bleeding from Nose: (Epistaxis) (Please see Chapter 10)

INFLUENZA

Causes: The climate and food which vitiate both vata and pitta produce this disease. It may be noted here that the tridosha (vata, pitta and kapha) is vitiated whenever there is a change in the season leading to this disease.

Symptoms: Dry cough with irritation of the nose, pharynx and larynx which causes bleeding from the nose, etc. If influenza is not treated at the initial stage it may lead on to a chronic stage involving the lungs. In Ayurveda it is termed as Vata Sleshmaka Jwara. In modern medicine influenza is said to be caused by a virus and it requires a minimum of 10 to 12 days to cure it. The temperature or fever may range between 101°F and 103°F. The patient will have a headeache, pain all over the body, sneezing, cold, a sore throat and is restless.

Treatment: The juice of orange is a cure for cold. One teaspoonful of dry Tulasi leaves should be taken and added to one litre of water and kept for an hour. After this period it should be filtered and given to the patient twice daily. Besides this, long pepper with honey, ginger juice with honey or 15 grains of Haridra (Curcumalonga) should be given to the patient twice daily along with warm milk to prevent complications of the lungs and to stimulate the liver. The best known remedy for influenza is Tribuvana Kirthi rasa or Naradhiya-Lakshmi Vilas which should be given in a dose of 2 tablets twice daily along with honey for a week. In the case of fever, ginger juice and the juice of Amritavalli (Tinospora cardifolia) half ounce each along with honey must be given to the patient twice daily. Mahasudarsha decoction is a useful remedy.

Diet: The patient should be given meat soups, vegetable soups which are bitter or sour along with a little quantity of garlic, camphor and warm water. He should not be exposed to the cold or take cold baths, live in a cold climate or eat fried foods.

HICCOUGH

Hiccough is an involuntary spasm of the glottis and the diaphragm. The resultant sounds produced by such a spasm is called Hiccough. In Ayurveda it is known as Hikka Roga and it is clinically divided into 5 types.

1) Maha Hikka
2) Gambhira Hikka
3) Vyapeta Hikka
4) Kshudra Hikka, and
5) Annaja Hikka

The first two are very serious and fatal and the remaining three are curable.

Causes: The Hikka is produced due to the following causes. Intake of undigested, heavy constipating dry food, milk and its products in excessive quantity, cold water, cold food, exposure to cold environment, fumes, sunlight, air, excessive exercise, walking long distances and suppression of natural urges like urine and faeces.

Symptoms: The patient will get a typical sound as Hikka. It is due to the obstruction of vata with phlegm. As a result of this, the sound is produced.

Treatment: Inhaling the fumes of fried bengal gram will stop Hikka immediately. Take 4 tolas of Shigru leaves, add it to 1 litre of water and heat. Kulattha about 3 tolas boiled and reduced to ¼ of its quantity should be given to the patient in the morning and evening. For Hikka of infants equal quantity of coconut and sugar candy (¼ gram plus ¼ gram) should be given. Ash of peacock feather is a well known remedy for Hiccough. Administering cold milk and hot milk alternatively will stop the disease or the Eladi vati which contains cardamom should be chewed 3 to 4 times a day. Psychotherapy is found to be very effective. Massaging the abdomen, with Ksheerabala Thaila and fomentation with a hot water bag, are found to be very effective. Bilvadi Lehya and Bilvadi vati are found to be very effective in practice.

Diet: A light diet like gruel and liquid diet are highly recommended. The causative factors should be avoided and if there is any constipation it should be relieved with Thriphala (½ TSF to 1 TSF) at bed time.

WHOOPING COUGH

Causes: The causes which are mentioned in Hiccough are also the casues for this disease. It is caused by an organism known as Bordetella pertusis. In the early stages, it starts with a running nose, watering in the eyes, irritation of the throat, sneezing, cough and fever. All the above symptoms will subside, with only cough which is paroxysmal in nature. It is usually expiratory in nature with a loud, sonorous inspiration called a Whoop. According to the Ayurvedic system of medicine, it is due to the vitiation of vata dosha in the body. Children are more prone to this disease; it is called Kukkasa or Dhustakasa.

Treatment: For the treatment of Vata take the juice of garlic, one teaspoon with ghee and honey; or the juice of Apamarga with honey one teaspoonful is found to be very effective. Prepared medicines like Dashamoola Ghritha, Agastyharitaki Rasayana, Kantakari Lehya and the juice of ginger with honey and castor oil to relieve constipation, should be given to the patient.

Diet: The same diet is to be followed as in the treatment of whooping cough. The patient must avoid cold food and cold climate.

BRONCHITIS

It is the inflammation of the bronchial tubes which usually carry air to the lungs. It may be acute or chronic. It may be due to primary causes or it may be secondary or other diseases.

Causes: When an individual inhales fumes or due to the vitiation of Vata, the food that we take will come up towards the oesophagus; either excessive exercise or consuming dry food will make the food go into the respiratory channel or inhibit sneezing, which is the Ayurvedic view. In Ayurveda bronchitis is called Kasa and is divided into five types: due to doshas like vata, pitta and kapha, due to injury and due to consumption. Kasa is a disease which starts due to defective digestion. In Kasa there is less oxygenation which in turn leads to excessive absorption of carbon dioxide. As a result of this, there is bluish colouration of the face, lips and nose. If the acute case is not treated properly, then it will lead to chronic bronchitis which may further result in chronic diseases of the lungs and pleura like turberculosis and asthma.

Treatment: If cough is present with phlegm then a powder of ginger, pepper, long pepper and Madhuyasti, must be mixed in equal quantity (5 grams each) and given to the patient in a dose of 4 grams twice daily with honey. To the juice of Amrutavalli (Tinospora cardifoli) equal quantity of honey should be added and given twice a day.

Unguentum: Take dry ginger in a dose of 5-30 grains or the paste of Bilva leaves and apply on the chest of the patient along with mustard seeds to get relief. To stop the cough take tender coconut water twice daily. However, if cough is present with excessive phlegm, then, the juice of vasa (Adathodavasia) must be taken along with honey, rock salt and Madhuyasti, twice daily.

If there is a dry cough associated with a burning sensation then give a tablet which is prepared from pepper, dry grapers and Madhuyasti. Even giving 30 grams of powder of Abaya with honey for a week will cure the cough. The Madhuyasti powder must be given to the patient in a dose 40 grams along with cow's milk twice daily. The prepared medicines used to cure the cough are:

1) Talisadi Vati
   Lavangadivati } Any one as lozenges 1 to 2 tabs a day.
   Eleadivati

2) Draksharista- 1 ounce + 1 ounce water twice daily.

3) Amrita Prashaghritha ITSF + milk twice daily especially in consumptive cough.

BRONCHIAL ASTHMA

It is characterised by paroxysmal dyspnoea associated with wheezing, due to the temporary narrowing of the bronchi, owing to the spasm of the muscle, mucosal swelling or viscid secretion. Allergy to fumes, dust, flowers, and pollen, ingestants like eggs, and milk and psychological disturbance are some of the causes as per modern system of medicine. According to Ayurveda it comes under Swasa and it is called Tamakaswasa. It is classified clinically into 5 types and "Tamaka Swasa" is one of them.

Causes: As already mentioned in "Hiccough".

Symptoms: The vitiated vata enters the "Pranavaha Srotas" (respiratory tract), head and neck, it brings the phlegm upwards and produces cold in the beginning. The patient will experience severe pain in the heart, difficulty in breathing, thirst, feeling of darkness and frequent cough. He will also have irritation in the throat and will find it difficult to talk and breathe. It is aggravated in a lying position and hence he will not get sleep. He will however feel more comfortable on sitting, and by taking hot food. His eyes will be projected, and there will be sweating on the forehead associated with dryness of the face. The dyspnoea will be more on taking cold water, inhaling cold air and taking food. One should take Chyavana Prasha Lahya constantly to get relief, as it will act as a preventive as well as a curative remedy.

Sitopaladi churan can also be taken in a dose of 30-40 grains along with Vasavalechya or Agastya Rasayana twice daily. Swasakutara Rasa should be taken in a dose of 200 m. grains twice daily with honey. It should not be taken by people who have weak hearts. For that purpose,

"Swasakasa Chintamani" should be taken in the above dosage itself. A known prescription for asthma consists of a mixture of Shringyadi churna 30 grains, Rasasindoora 200 m. grams and Abhraka bhasma 200 m. grams which should be taken twice daily along with the juice of Apamarga (Achyaranthus aspera) and Vasa (Adhatoda vasica). Pepper longum can also be take in a dose 30 grains twice daily, with Kanakasava half to one ounce as per the direction of the Ayurvedic physician.

Diet: The decoction prepared from Kulattha (horse gram) or dry grapes is very useful. Light food like gruel prepared with Trikastu (Pepper longum, Pepper nigrum, Zingeber officinalis) can be given depending upon the patient's digestive capacity. One should not smoke

Vasa (Lat: Adhatoda Vasica)

or expose oneself to rain and cold wind. Besides, the patient should avoid curd, buttermilk, banana and fried things. For such patients alcoholic preparations are strictly prohibited.

HAEMOPTYSIS

Definition: It is a process by which blood is coughed out from the lungs. It is mainly due to either tuberculosis or cancer of the lungs. In Ayurveda it is one of the variety of "Raktapitta", a haemorrhagic disorder. It is otherwise called "Urdhwaga Raktapitta".

Cause: Haemoptysis is caused due to the following factors: excessive exposure to sunlight, excessive exercise, walking too much, coitus, eating the following in excessive quantity: acute hot, alkaline, saltish, sour and pungent foods. The pitta is vitiated and throws the blood from the upper or lower part of the body or through the hair follicles.

Symptoms: Coughing of blood by the patient either with mucus or without it.

Treatment: The famous remedy for Raktapitta is "Vasa" (Adhatoda vasica) usually given in the form of juice in a dose of half an ounce or one ounce with honey and Laksha. It may be noted that the juice will be bitter, therefore, it is better if it is taken with honey. Khanda Kooshmanda Lehya should be taken in a dose of one teaspoonful twice daily with milk, so also Vasavalehya can be taken. Chandrakala rasa can be given 1 tablet thrice daily along with 10 grains of Pravala Pishti (preparation of coral) with honey.

Diet: The factors that are mentioned in the causation of the disease must be totally avoided along with alcohol, horse gram (Kulattha) etc., old rice, cold water, dry grapes, soup of patola (Bittergourd), meat soup and mudga (green gram) etc.

HOARSENESS OF VOICE

Hoarseness of voice is produced due to the inflammation of the throat either due to laryngitis (i.e., inflammation of the larynx) or due to the inflammation of the pharynx.

Causes: It is caused by taking cold and hot things alternatively, excessive speaking like recitation of mantras. It is clinically classified into six types and may be due to the abnormal growth and tuberculosis or cancer of the larynx.

Treatment: To a piece of ginger add about 5 grains of asafoetida (Hingu). The grains should be kept inside the ginger and covered by red soil; it should be burnt in low fire till the smell of ginger is obtained. Then it should be removed from the fire, a tablet is to be made and it should be swallowed. Eladi vati or Khadiradi vati chewed three or four times a day will improve the tone. Even administering Vacha (Acorus calamus) or Yasti Madhu, Churna (Glyrrhiza glabra) will benefit. The patient should be given a laxative like Triphala to remove constipation.

Diet: Dry grapes, cow's ghee, ginger and pepper must be taken with hot water or honey. It is better to avoid sour, cold, fried things and curd. The patient should also not expose himself to cold climate.

TUBERCULOSIS

Tuberculosis is caused by an organism called "Mycobactirium Tuberculosis", in which the patient will have cough, with or without sputum, evening rise of temperature, loss of weight and loss of appetite. In Ayurveda it is called "Rajayakshma" (King of diseases). It is a disease wherein there will be complete emaciation of the tissues, hence, it is called "shosha". There will be spitting of blood with or without mucus.

Causes: Suppression of natural urges, excessive exercise, fasting too much, and psychological causes like jealousy, grief, anger and excessive coitus. It is a disease predominant of phlegm.

Symptoms: The patient will have pain in the shoulder region, sides of the chest, burning sensation in the hands and feet, fever, loss of appetite, difficulty in breathing, coughing out of blood, hoarseness of voice pain all over the body and diarrhoea.

Treatment: Food which is highly nutritious must be given to the patient. He should take fresh air and therefore be kept in a good ventilated place. That is why sanatoriums are constructed in a good environment.

Yasti churna (Glyrrihiza glabra) should be administered in dosage of 30-40 gains along with honey and ghee in different proportions. It has been found very effective in the dry, hacking cough of tuberculosis.

If the phlegm is too much then the juice of vasa should be given in a dose of 3 teaspoonful along with honey and trikatu.

Whenever there is blood in the sputum, then Yasti Churna with Laksha and the juice of vasa should be administered to the patient for at least 15 days to 1 month, or a decoction prepared from Trikatu, Amalaki and Atimadhura and Amrita vati should be administered for the same period of time. Chyavanaprasha or Kooshamanda Lehya should be given 1 teaspoonful twice daily along with cow's milk. It will not only improve the digestive system, but also tone up the tissues of the body. Amalaki and Pippali are also present in the Chyavanaprasha preparation. Prepared medicines like Mahalakshmi Vilas rasa should be administered in a dose of 200 mg. twice daily along with Draksharista one ounce, if a cavity is present in the lungs.

Diet: The diet should consist of vegetables like bittergourd (Trichosanthes dioica) and drumstick, masha, cow's milk, raddish, wheat, old rice, blackgram, and light diet.

Meat soup, prepared with Piper longum, barley, horsegram, and dry ginger, is very useful. One should avoid curd, buffalo, milk, heavy and starchy food, sweet foods, cold water, excessive coitus and dry sleeping and night vigil.

TONSILITIS (GALAYU)

Tonsils are situated behind the tongue on either side of the pharynx. It is a round mass consisting mainly of lymphoid tissues. Its inflammation is mainly caused by "Haemolytic Streptococus". According to the Ayurvedic system of medicine it is called "Tundikeri or Galayu".

Signs and Symptoms: Owing to the vitiation of kapha and rakta a mass of the size of a big amalaki which is stable and with excessive pain will be produced in the throat. It obstructs the intake of food, and produces constipation. The patient also experiences frequent attacks of cold before the onset of this disease.

Treatment: Two Detonsytabs twice daily with Detonsy paint must be used. Hot unguentum (lepa) which is prepared with Harithaki must be applied; or a paste made out of the powder of Madhuyasti (Glyrrihiza glabra) and Vacha (Acoruscalamus) with honey, mixed with Tankana (Borax). Khadiradi vati or Lavangadi vati or Talisadi vati must be given to the patient to be used as lozenges 3 to 4 times a day. In chronic cases Agastya Haritaki Rasayana must be taken internally in a dose of 1 teaspoonful with honey. Abhaya with honey can be applied on the tonsils for relief.

Diet: Liquid diet like gruel which is warm must be given to the patient. Vegetable soup prepared form "Kulattha" (Dolichos biflorus), mudga (Phasolusmungo), bittergourd, and raddish etc., should be given. Meat soup can be given prepared with vegetables like bittergourd, patola and raddish. The patient is advised to avoid heavy, hard, dry, sour food, including curd, milk and sugarcane juice.

Other Regimens: The patient must not sleep during the day and must keep his bowels clear with Triphala. Bathing is restricted.

4

CARDIO-VASCULAR HAEMOPOETIC SYSTEMS:Diseases and Remedies

ANAEMIA

Causes and Symptoms: It is due to the deficiency of nutritional food, it is also due to defective blood formation, e.g., drugs. Anaemia may be pernicious or aplastic anaemia. Iron deficiency anaemia is very common. There are another two types of anaemia depending on whether the size of the red blood corpuscles is macrocytic or microcytic (big or small). In Ayurveda, as it produces pallor in the body, it is called Pandu and is classified clinically into 5 types: Pittaja, Vataja, Kaphaja, Sannipataja and Mridbakshanaja. The treatment lies in improving the blood condition of the patient and in stopping the causes for the destruction of red blood corpuscles, by adding proper food, proper blood, vitamins and iron, etc. Iron preparations which are advocated in the treatment of anaemia must be given to the patient. Due to less quantity of blood in the body, the patient feels weak. Paleness in the face is noticeable. There will be an increase in heart rate and pulse rate.

Treatment: The treatment of anaemia consists of snehana karma. For this purpose either Dadimadya Ghrita or Pancha Tikta Ghrita must be given in a dose of one ounce per day and Sodhana or laxatives as Trivrit churna or Triphala churna. These come under poorva karma or the pre-operative procedure. The main treatment or the operative procedure lies in the administration of medicines like Navayasa churna in a dose of 30 to 40 grs.twice daily with honey and buttermilk, Lohasava with Kaseesa Bhasma (one ounce with 200 mg.).

Punarnava Mandura can be given in the dose of 30 grs. twice daily with milk or buttermilk.

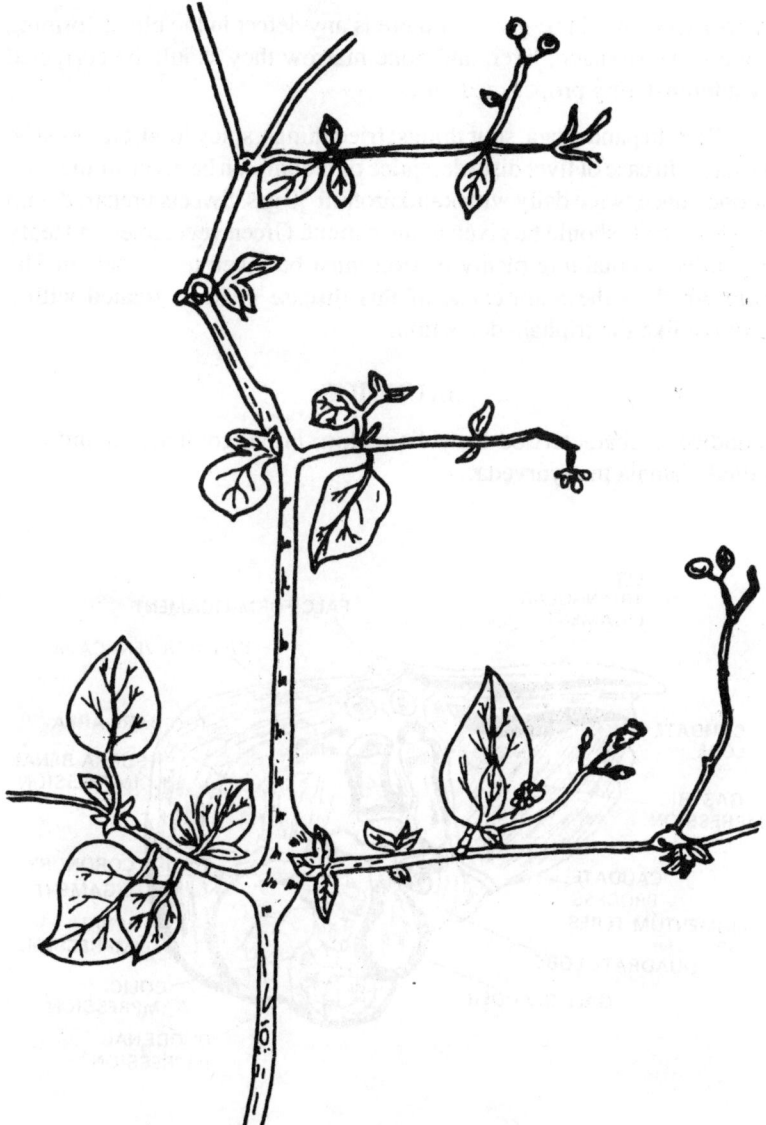

Punarnava (Lat. Boerhaavia diffusa)

If there is any bleeding from the mouth, nose, lungs, etc., due to injury, piles or other causes, they should be immediately attended to :

Proper food should be given. If there is any defect in the blood-forming organs like stomach, liver, and bone marrow they should be corrected by administering proper medicines.

Diet: In panduroga, sour things, fried things, spicy food, etc. must be avoided. In case of liver disordersjuice of brahmi can be given in the dose of one ounce twice daily with katukarohini 30 grs. Sweets prepared with gingelly seeds should be given to the patient. Green vegetables and leafy vegetables containing plenty of iron must be given to the patient.The pitta which is the main cause of this disease must be treated with a laxative like the triphala decoction.

JAUNDICE

Jaundice is characterised by yellow skin, urine, conjunctiva and it is called Kamala in Ayurveda.

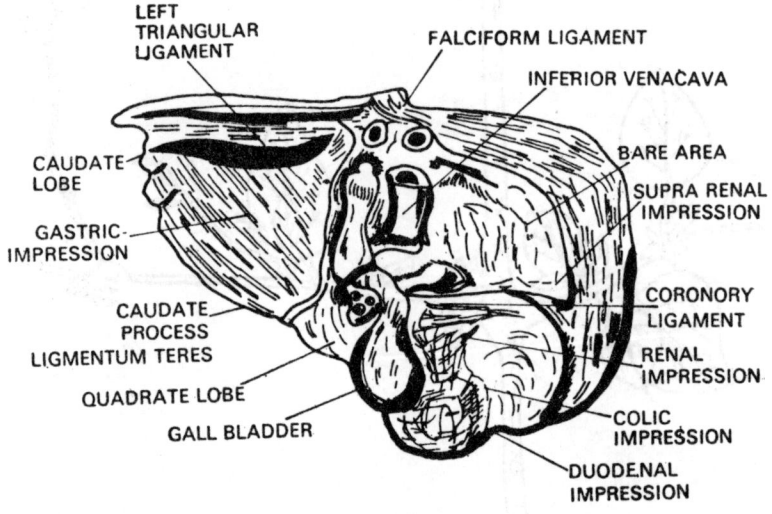

Liver

Causes: This is nothing but a yellowish colouration appearing all over the body including the eyes, skin, and urine. This is due to the excessive circulation of bile pigments in the blood. Bile is produced by the liver and normally it is thrown out through the urine and faeces. But if there is an obstruction in the bile duct, bile gets absorbed into the blood circulation and hence the yellow colouration in the body. In case of obstruction of the bile duct the motion will be clay-coloured or pale white in colour. But urine will be excessively yellowish in all cases of jaundice.

All the causes that produce anaemia will also cause jaundice.

Signs and Symptoms: There will be yellowish colour in the skin and eyes associated with weakness and defective digestion of fatty food. There will be excessive destruction of red blood corpuscles due to many causes like leukemia or any other haemolytic disorder of the blood. A generalised itching all over the body will be experienced.

Treatment: In Ayurveda, for any pitta disorder the main treatment would be to give a laxative. Katukarohini (Picrorrhiza kurora) and Trivrit (Operculina turpethum) are to be administered (one teaspoonful each along with hot water) in the morning depending upon the condition of the patient and severity as well as stage of the disease. Arogyavardinivati contains katuki as a major ingredient and Avipathikara churna contains Trivrit as a major constituent. In some cases Aragvadha (Cassia fistula) should be administered with castor oil once daily. Early in the morning a teaspoonful of Vasaka (Adhatoda vasica) along with 2 teaspoonful of Gudoochi (Tinospora cardifolia) should be given along with a teaspoonful of honey. The juice of Bhumyamalaki (Phyllanthus niruri)is a famous remedy administered to all types of jaundice. In case of obstructive jaundice the pulp of aloes should be given in a dose of 2 teaspoons twice daily.

Liv-52 tablets or Livomyn tablets can be given in a dose of two tablets thrice daily for adults. Even the decoction of triphala (Haritaki, Bibhitaki and Amalaki) an ounce twice daily will cure the disease. Navayasa churna can be given to patients in a dose of 300mg. with honey twice daily.

Diet and Regimens: All sweet things like orange juice, sugarcane juice, grape juice are advised as they neutralise the bile pigments in blood and induce urination.

Bitter vegetables and sour pomegranate are advised to be taken. Meat soups are also advocated in this condition. Buttermilk with old rice is a specific diet for the patient. Sour vegetables, pungent food, spicy food, salty food, must be strictly avoided. Alcohol should not be given to the patient at any cost. The patient should be made to rest in bed and should avoid sex, sugar, excitement and emotion, heat and sun, etc.

CIRRHOSIS OF THE LIVER

Cirrhosis of the liver is a term used for chronic diffused liver disease due to many causes with destruction of parenchymal cells, with distortion of the normal labular architecture with nodular regeneration of the parenchymal cells associated with overgrowth of fibrous tissue. In short, it is nothing but an internal inflammation of the liver.

The liver is one of the important organs of the body as it plays a vital role in the digestion, metabolism and other important physiological functions of the body.

In children and in adults it is called infective cirrhosis of the liver.
Signs and Symptoms: In the case of cirrhosis of the liver in children, the following signs and symptoms are produced.

Pain is noticed in the upper portion of the right part of the abdomen (liver area) due to pressure of the enlarged liver and the lungs produce cough and there is difficulty in breathing. Sometimes a sensation of vomiting is observed. After some time the patient will get relief from cough and difficulty in respiration, due to the shrinking of the liver. The child may complain of loss of weight. The liver tissue will become fibrosed and due to the obstruction of venous circulation water will accumulate in the abdomen. And the patient will notice distension of abdomen, cough, difficulty in breathing and loss of appetite.

Treatment: Cirrhosis of the liver is mainly due to defective diet and in adults it is commonly due to excessive intake of alcohol. The liver detoxicates the toxins that are produced in the body or due to drugs and foods. Whenever it fails to detoxicate and neutralise the toxins, cirrhosis of the liver is produced. The patient must be advised to give up coffee, tea, alcoholic drinks and food containing poisonous material. The following single drugs can be tried successfully on a liver cirrhosis patient. When a patient is suffering from jaundice he should be treated with the decoction of Triphala or the juice of Amrithavalli one ounce early in the morning for a period of 7-10 days, with Arogyavardhini: 2 tablets twice daily. It will not only cure the jaundice but also protect the liver from cirrhosis.

Katuka Rohini (Picrrhiza kurrora) is the drug of choice for cirrhosis in adults. The root or rhizome of this plant is indicated as a medicine here. It is bitter in taste and grows in the Himalayas. This can be administered in a dose of 30-40 grains along with honey twice daily to an adult male Whenever there is constipation then its dose should be doubled. It is a powerful chologogue and acts as a purgative by virtue of increasing the bile from the liver indirectly. If congestion of the bile is reduced then liver tissues will start functioning.

Arogyavardhini is a famous drug for cirrhosis of the liver. It not only contains Katukarohini in sufficient proportions but also copper in the form of Bhasma. Copper helps in the formation of blood. It can be given in the tablet form in doses of two tablets twice daily (one tablet 0.25 grams), depending upon the gravity of the liver damage and seriousness of the condition of the patient . Another drug of choice is Bhringaraja (Eclipta alba) which is a small herb with white, yellow or blue flowers and which grows in marshy places.The juice of the blue flowers is used in medicine. For children below 10 years half or one teaspoonful of this juice can be administered twice daily. It should always be administered with honey as it is bitter and astringent in taste.

Diet: The patient must be given vegetables which are bitter in taste, like Patola, bittergourd and bitter variety of drumstick. Cow's milk with rice should be taken, goat's or camel's milk may be substituted in place of cow's milk. The patient must take salt-free, fat-free and curd-free diet. Buttermilk can be used in plenty. Rock salt may be used in place of ordinary salt. Whenever there is accumulation of fluid in the abdomen the patient must be given a gruel prepared with Panchakola as a medicine. The decoction prepared from Dashamoola, Panchakola, Triphala and Trivrit can be administered in a dose of one ounce twice daily. The above drugs should be taken in the proportion of 10 grams each mixed with one litre of water and heated and reduced to one-fourth (250 mls) its quantity.

Other Regimens: The patient is advised bed rest. He must not sleep during the day or keep awake at night. He should not do any risky exercise.

SCURVY

It is a condition wherein there will be haemorrhage which is muco-cutaneous in nature associated with anaemia, spongy gums and weakness.

Causes: It is due to the deficiency of Vitamin C in the food. Vitamin C is present in fresh ripe fruits like Amalaki (Emblica officinalis) which is present in abundant quantity in Chyavanaprasha Linctus.

Signs and Symptoms: There will be bleeding associated with foul smell and reddish colouration in the gums with little oozing. It is caused by kapha and rakta (phlegm and blood).

Treatment: Vitamin C in the form of Amalaki should be given along with leafy vegetables, pomegranate (Dadima) and Bilva (Aegle marmelos). The patient should not be exposed to excessive heat.

HAEMORRHAGE

The circulation of blood in human beings was first demonstrated about 5000 years ago by an Indian surgeon 'Sushruta'. It is recorded in his *Sushruta Samhita*.

Any bleeding from any part of the body is called Haemorrhage.

Causes: The following causes produce vitiation of pitta and rakta and thereby bring about haemorrhage in the body, viz., intake of acute, hot, alkaline, sour and pungent food, exposure to heat, doing excessive exercise and walking too much. In Ayurveda it is called "Raktapitta" and it is clinically classified into 3 types.

The bleeding may occur either from the artery or vein. It may occur from the mouth or it may occur in the form of passing of blood from the lower part of the body as in piles or colitis.

Treatment: Ayurvedic theory postulates not to check the bleeding immediately as it may cause fainting, loss of appetite and fever, etc. In vomiting of blood, the juice of Amalaki with Vasa in a dose of 2 teaspoonful each can be administered twice daily: Kooshmanda and Pravala Pishti are to be given in a dose of one teaspoonful twice daily with 20 grains respectively. In case of bleeding from the anus the patient must be given 2 teaspoonful of Kutajarishta twice daily or Mocha Rasa with milk alongwith Chandrakalrasa or Pittantakarasa twice daily. In the case of bleeding from the vagina, the patient must be given 2 teaspoonful of Ashokarista with 2 tablets of Chandrakalarasa twice daily. In case of bleeding through the urethra Chandanasava or Usheerasava or juice of Gokshura and Shatavari with Shilajit (1 ounce + 200 mg.) with Saribadyasava 1 teaspoonful twice daily alongwith Pravala Bhasma in a dose of 200 mg. may be given.

Diet: Cold water and cold juice prepared from dry grapes, pomegranates, dates, apple, oranges, coconut water, sugarcane juice and non-irritating vegetables should be eaten. If the bleeding is internal, there will be palpitation, profuse sweating and thready pulse. The patient should consult the doctor immediately. He should be given bed rest and should stay in a cool and calm atmosphere.

HYPERTENSION

The heart is a vital organ of our body which propels the blood to all the systems through the arteries of the body. The blood is passed through the arterial vessels which are elastic in nature. Blood pressure is nothing but the pressure exerted by it on the vessel walls. There are two types of blood pressure: systolic and diastolic. Systolic blood pressure is that pressure which is exerted by the blood in the walls of the arteries during the contractive phase of the heart; diastolic blood pressure is that pressure which is exerted by the blood on its vessel walls during the expansive phase of the heart. Normally the blood pressure increases during emotion, excitement and anger and is low during sleep and rest. It varies from individual to individual depending upon age, sex, mental and physical work of the individual.

Causes: Taking dry and cold food, too much exercises, mental exertion, keeping late nights, excessive use of alcohol, irregularity in taking food and excessive salt will cause vitiation of vata.

Hypertension may be "functional or essential". It may be due to the thickening of the arterial wall (Arterio-Sclerosis) especially in old age or it may be due to stress and strain as in "functional hypertension". Disorders of the kidney may also produce an "essential hypertension".

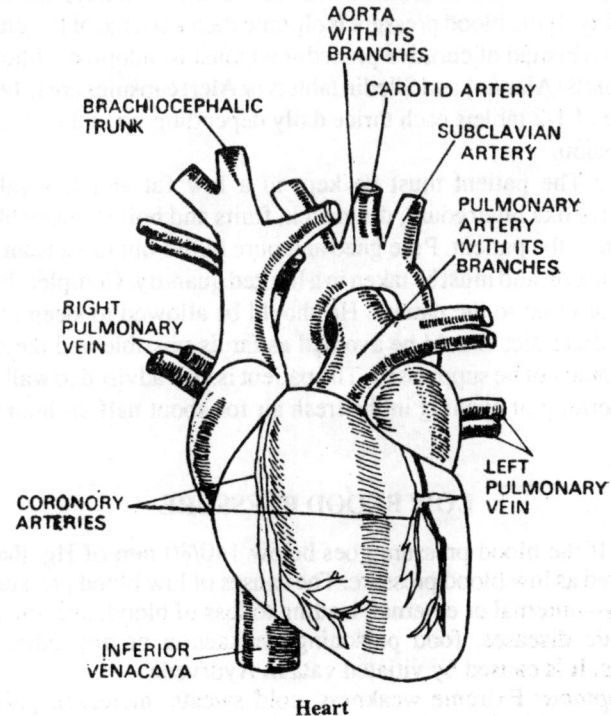

Heart

Symptoms: Headache, weakness, giddiness, sleeplessness, palpitation, and disorders in digestion are some of the important symptoms. If the blood pressure is not controlled immediately it may cause not only defective vision but also a cerebral stroke leading to paralysis and death.

Treatment: The treatment of hypertension depends on its proper diagnosis. If it is due to secondary causes, then such causes should be traced and treated properly.

One teaspoonful of onion juice with honey should be taken for 15-20 days to bring the blood presure down to normal; or garlic (Allivum sattivum) with Draksha (Vitis vinfera) 20 grains each, boiled in a cup of milk and three cups of water reducing the whole to 1 cup. Half of it should be given in the morning and evening for 15 days to 1 month till the blood pressure is brought to normal. Garlic has the property of reducing vata whereas Draksha alleviates pitta in the system. Sarpagandha can be given in a dose of 20 grains twice daily with the powder of the bark of Arjuna (Terminalia arjuna) in the same dose. Shankhapusphi and Brahmi juice one teaspoonful each at bedtime with cow's milk will keep the brain in tranquillity. If the blood pressure is chronic then a course of Panchakama treatment (Pentad of curative procedures) must be adopted without fail. Arjin tablets (Alarsin) and Siledin tablets or Alert capsules are to be given in a dose of 1-2 tablets each thrice daily depending upon the severity of hypertension.

Diet: The patient must be kept in a low fat and low salt diet. Vegetables like bittergourd, drumstick, fruits and boiled vegetables can be givien to the patient. Pure ghee and pure butter obtained from cow's milk are useful and must be taken in a limited quantity. Complete bed rest must be advised to the patient. He should be allowed to sleep at night. Carbohydrate diet should be avoided as far as possible and the natural urges should not be suppressed. The patient is also advised to walk either in the morning or evening in the fresh air for about half-an-hour to one hour.

LOW BLOOD PRESSURE

Causes: If the blood pressure goes below 140/80 mm of Hg. then it is considered as low blood pressure. The causes of low blood pressure may be injury—internal or external, leading to loss of blood, anaemia, acute or chronic diseases, food poisoning, leukaemia or any other blood disorders. It is caused by vitiated vata in Ayurveda.

Symptoms: Extreme weakness, cold sweats, increased pulse and heart rate, giddiness and history of fainting, headache, and chest pain.

Treatment: The causes must be treated properly, i.e., the vitiation of vata should be treated and brought to normal. Dashamoolarista, Ashwagandharista 1 teaspoonful thrice daily with equal quantity of water and meat soup obtained from the flesh of chicken, rabbit and goat, or the soups of meat and black gram, apple, grapes and beans of all varieties may also be given. He is advised to take a highly nutritive and strengthening diet with light exercise.

LEUKAEMIA (BLOOD CANCER)

It is a condition wherein there is a destruction of red blood corpuscles with an increase of white blood corpuscles. It is otherwise called "Cancer of the blood" in its chronic stage. In Ayurveda it is called "Vatolbana Sannipataja Pandu Roga" wherein all the signs and symptoms of anaemia will be present. The causes of leukaemia are the same as the causes which lead to anaemia. However, in leukaemia, there may also be haemorrhage from the nose, gums, stomach and the bowels; there will be diarrhoea associated with fever and enlargement of the spleen and glands of the body. The patient may also feel difficulty in breathing.

Treatment: It is a challenge to the modern system of medicine as it has not been able to treat this disease successfully; but Ayurveda believes that it is caused due to the vitiation of tridoshas (vata, pitta, kapha) and therefore if these tridoshas are brought to normal with the medicines which are indicated in Ayurveda, then the patient will be able to get a cure. The following medicines can be given:

Chandrasooryatmakarasa, Trilokasundararasa and Dravyadilehya, etc. The ashes of diamond (Vajra Bhasma) or Heeraka Bhasma in a dose of 5-6 mgs. with or without Mukta Pisti and Pravala can be given. Panchamritarasa is also useful.

In some of the cases where the liver gets enlarged with severe anaemia, Pravala Panchamritarasa with Yakrit Pleyodararirasa along with Vajra Bhasma, each in a dose of 200 mgs. with 6 mgs. of Vajra Bhasma respectively can be given twice daily. In the chronic stages these can be given along with the juice of Bhringaraj and turmeric. Fresh liver juice can also be given intermittently.

Diet: Old rice, bittergourds, raddish, oranges, grapes, goat meat soup, cow's milk, buttermilk and ghee. Ayurveda has advocated the use of either the blood of goat or rabbit 1 to 2 ounce at a time. Sometimes blood transfusion of other persons can be given. Blood matching must be done before blood transfusion takes place.

5

FEVERS AND THEIR REMEDIES

Fever can be defined as a condition where there is an increase in temperature of the body. It is called Jwara in Ayurveda. Generally the temperature of a normal healthy body ranges between 98.4°F and 99.5°F. If the temperature rises beyond 106°F, then it is considered to be Hyperpyrexia and if it goes beyond 107°F or 108°F then death is certain.

Signs and Symptoms: There will be an arrest of sweating, and an affliction of excessive heat and the patient will feel a sensation of contraction in his body.The entire symptoms will be present in fever. They are termed as general symptoms.

Types of Fevers

There are 32 types of fevers depending upon the vitiation of tridoshas, change of seasons, and vitiation of blood.This is according to Charaka, the well known author of *Charaka Samhita*—a medical treatise on Ayurveda. But according to modern medicine there are about 25 varieties of fevers.

COMMON FEVERS

When a patient has fever, pain all over the body and arrest of sweating, then it is termed as common fever without any known cause.

Treatment: Generally in the initial stage of the fever the patient must be kept on a fast or must be given only light gruel. And in the middle of the fever, medicines which have the property of digestion and assimilation must be given. In the last stage of the fever mild laxatives may be administered. The patient must be given a decoction prepared from Musta, Parpashtaka, Dhanyaka and Amrutavalli, each drug should be taken in a dose of 1 teaspoonful or added to half litre of pure water which must then be boiled and reduced to one-fourth proportion. This should be administered thrice daily, or even the juice of Tulasi one teaspoonful with 10 grains of pepper and administered along with honey.

The following prescriptions hold good for the common type of fevers:

1. Maha Mrutyunjaya rasa: 200 mg. with Pravala Bhasma: 200 mg. with honey or Guduchi juice or Amritarishta (half ounce twice daily).

2. Guduchi satva: half gm.
   Tribhuvana Keerti: 200 mg.
   Mahasudarshana churna-4 gms.

The prescription given above has to be taken thrice daily along with honey or with hot water.

TYPHOID FEVER

When a patient has a step-ladder fashion of fever then it is called enteric or typhoid fever. It affects the intestines and hence it is called *Antrika jwara* in Ayurveda.

Signs and Symptoms: Frontal headache, loss of sleep and an evening rise of temperature. The fever reaches its maximum on the 8th day and sometimes it runs up to 24-28 days. The peculiarity of this fever is that the pulse rate does not increase with the rise in temperature. Usually for every degree of raise of temperature there must be an increase of pulse rate. But it is not seen in this type of fever. The patient will have the following abdominal symptoms also: loose motions, pain and gurgling sounds, distension of the abdomen, and ulceration in intestines. Later he may develop peritonitis and perforation as complications.

Treatment

1. Amritarishta: One ounce
   Laghu Malini Vasanta: 200 mg. } Thrice daily with hot
   Sudarshana Churna: 4 gms. water or honey.
   Maha Mrutyunjaya: 200 mg.

   or

2. Guduchi satva: ½ gm.
   Lakshminarayana rasa: 200 mg. } Thrice daily with
   Mahajwarankusha rasa: 200 mg. hot water or honey.
   (Chandraputi) Pravala bhasma: 200 mg.

In Ayurveda, Antrika Sannipatajwara is produced due to the vitiation of tridoshas and the prescription given above is suitable. In the last stage of the disease Indukantha Ghritham two teaspoonful thrice daily with milk is a specific remedy.

Diet: The patient must be given Shadanga Paniya prepared out of:

1. Mustaka (Cyperus rotandus)
2. Parpastaka (Fumeriaparviflora)
3. Ushira (Vetiveria zizanoidis)
4. Chandana (Santalum album)
5. Udicochya (Coriandrum sativum)
6. Nagara (Gingiber officinale)

and administered as a drink instead of water.

Only liquid diet like gruel prepared from fried rice or suji can be administered.

RHEUMATIC FEVER

The patient will have a cold associated with swelling and pain in the joints. It is called Amavatajwara in Ayurveda. It can afflict children as well as adults.

Signs and Symptoms: The patient will have a cold associated with fever and pain and swelling in major joints like knees, elbows and ankles. With the rise of temperature to 102-103°F, the patient will have pain in the body, loss of taste, thirst, loss of appetite and laziness and heaviness in the body.

Treatment: According to the modern system of medicine, rheumatic fever is caused by some infective organisms and therefore will be treated with some antibodies; but in Ayurveda it is due to the derangement of digestive fire and hence that should be toned up properly to correct the disease.

The following treatment can be observed:

1. Arogyavardhini 1 tablet (of 120 mg.) ⎫ Thrice daily
    Maharasnadi Quatha: 1 ounce ⎬ with hot water
    Yogaraja Churna: 1 gm. ⎭ or honey.

2. Draksharishta: ½ ounce
    Amritarishta: ½ ounce ⎫ Thrice daily
    Amavatarirasa (200 mg.) ⎬ with honey.
    Bhringaraja Churna: ¼ gm. ⎭

3. Rasna Ghrita: 2 teaspoonful thrice daily in chronic cases.

The juice of Guduchi 1 ounce with powder of dry ginger 15 grains twice daily.

External Treatment: Massaging of the body with oils is contra-indicated in this condition. However, Amavathahara taila (Impcops) or Kottumchukadi taila (Arya Vaidya Sala, Kottakal) can be applied all over the body. It should be suitably warmed.

Valuka Sweda: Sufficient quantity of sand is taken and a bolus is prepared; it is warmed over a hot plate and fomentation is given to the swollen joints. The patient will get relief from the pain and swelling in the joints.

Diet: A gruel from fried rice with the decoction of milk and Panchakola must be prepared and given to the patient twice daily.Rest in bed and fluids, diuretics, and laxatives and bittergourd, are all recommended. To remove constipation Triphala can be given; to tone up the liver Katuki can be given in a dose of 30 grains twice daily.

MALARIA

It is an intermittent type of fever caused by a parasite of the plasmodium group.It is produced by the bite of an Anopheles (a type of mosquito). The fever is spread all over the world and the temperature may be seen regularly, on alternate days or on second days. It may run into a chronic stage if it is not treated soon.

Signs and Symptoms: The patient will have liver and spleen enlargement, fever, headache, pain in the abdomen, vomiting and delirium.

Treatment: A decoction must be prepared out of Mahasudarshana churna; add Mahajwarankusha (200 mg.) and Pravala Bhasma (200 mg.) and administer it twice daily.

A decoction prepared out of following drugs can be given in a dose of 2 teaspoon twice daily: (1) Sahadevi (Vernonia cineria), (2) Saptaparna (Alstonia scholaris), (3) Karanja (Caesal pinia bondu cella), (4) Tulasi (Ocimum sanctum), (5) Kirata Tikta (Swertia chirata), (6) Drona Puspi (Leweas cephalotes, (7) Karavellaka (Momordia charantia), (8) Trayamana (Gentiana kurroa).

If there is more heat along with temperature, then Chirayita, bark of Saptaparna, Ushira and black Jeeraka should be mixed and taken along with honey in a dose of 2 teaspoonful. If there is cold along with fever then one-fourth teaspoonful of Katuki or Nimba bark should be added to the above decoction and administered to the patient. Root of Lata Karanja should be cleaned and prepared in the form of dry powder to be given in a dose of half gm. along with honey.

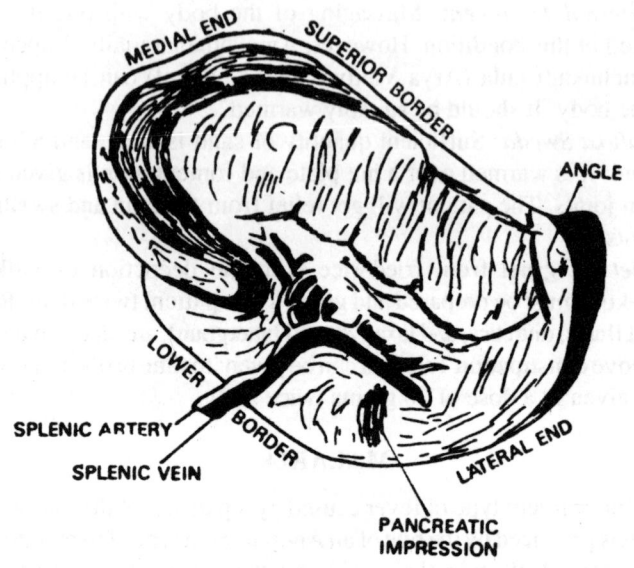

Spleen

FILARIA

Filaria is a disease caused by the bite of wuchereria bancrofti—a type of mosquito. Filaria is also called Elephantiasis. In Ayurveda it is known as Sleepada. There will be solid oedema in the skin of the leg and scrotum and the skin will resemble the skin of an elephant.

Causes: It spreads through adulterated and contaminated drinking water containing female worm—like species. It is very common in Karnataka, especially in the coastal areas like Mangalore in Cochin and Travancore in southern India and other states like Bihar, Bengal and Uttar Pradesh in northern India.

Signs and Symptoms: Fever with rigor continues up to 4 days and it is caused due to the vitiation of kapha. According to Ayurveda there will be swelling of the scrotum and swelling in the legs.

Treatment

1. Sleepadari rasa (200 mg.) or Nityananda rasa (200 mg.) with Lodhrasava (½ ounce) twice daily with an equal quantity of water for about two or three months will give relief to the patient.

2.   Sleepada Gaja Kesari rasa, 200 mg. with Sanjeevani Vati (200 mg.) with Lodhrasava one ounce + Pippali Churna (½ gram).

BLACK WATER FEVER

It is called Kalamasha Jwara in Ayurveda. A patient suffering from this disease will pass haemoglobin in the urine. Haemoglobin is present in RBC (Red Blood Corpuscles). After it breaks it will be reutilised for the formation of RBC. There will be a reddish tinge to the urine. It occurs in India, Central Africa and other tropical countries. It also occurs as a complication of quinine therapy.

Signs and Symptoms: The patient will experience a rise in temperature, around 104°-105°F with reddish or blackish urine, nausea, vomiting, shivering and jaundice. The liver and spleen are usually enlarged. Initially the temperature starts and later stops with profuse sweating, jaundice and emaciation. It is produced due to the vitiation of vāta and kapha according to Ayurveda.

Treatment: The patient must be given sufficient quantity of fluids and a nutritive diet. Sarjakshara with lemon juice and sugar is a good drink. The patient should be given the following medicines:

(1)   Guduchi Satva (½ gm.), Laksha churna (½ gm.), Pravala Bhasma, Narayana Vati (2 tablets) twice daily with honey.

(2)   Lohasava (½ ounce) twice daily.
     Vishamajwarantaka Rasa (200 gms) twice daily.

(3)   Shatavari: ½ gm.   with milk one cup twice daily.
     Gokshura: ½ gm.
     + Laksha: 400 mg. }   twice daily

(4)   Chandra Prabhavati and
     Chandrakala rasa 2 tablets each twice daily.

KALA AZAR

It is called Kala Jwara in Ayurveda and Black Disease in Assam. It is also known by different names like Dum-Dum fever, Black Fever and visceral leishmaniasis. It also occurs in Sudan and Africa, due to the bite of the sand fly—Philebotomus argentipes.

Signs and Symptoms: The onset of fever will be irregular, with anaemia and enlargement of the spleen. The WBC (White Blood Corpuscles) are less in count. The fever continues for 3-6 weeks and it recurs always with the enlargement of liver and spleen alongwith black spots on the forehead, palms, soles of the feet and face. There may be distension of the stomach with emaciation associated with pain in the bones of the legs and arms.

Treatment: In modern medicine Antimony preparations are used. Probably it may have been influenced by Ayurveda because even in Ayurveda Antimony is used as Shuddha Neelanjana in the dose of 100 mg. with Pravala Bhasma, Tamra Bhasma each 100 mgs. alongwith Yakrit Pleehodarari Loha (100 mg). Another remedy is:

Shuddha Neelanjana (100 mg.) with Amritarishta (½ ounce) with Loha Bhasma (100 mg.) + Katuki Churna (40 grains) twice daily.

HECTIC FEVER

It is called Pralepaka Jwara in Ayurveda. It occurs either in septic poisoning, tuberculosis or any chronic illness.

Symptoms: The temperature will come down at night and generally ranges from 102 to 104°F.The patient may have profuse sweating with weakness after fever. This is due to the vitiation of vata and pitta.

Treatment: Vasanta Malati Rasa (100 mg.), Guduchi Satva (½ gm), Stiophaladi Churna (½ gm), Pravalabhasma (100 mg.) thrice daily with honey.

In case of Septicemia and Pyogenic conditions the following prescription is found to be successful:

(a) Sarvana Sundara Rasa (200 mg.) + Katuki Churna (1 gm).
(b) Sanjeevani Vati (200 mg.) + Panchakola Churna (20grs.) + Punarnava (½gm).

If the heart is involved then Hridayarnava Rasa (200 mg.) with Shringa Bhasma (200 mg.) must be administered twice daily with honey.

MENINGITIS

It is known as Mastishka Shotha in Ayurveda. It is mostly due to tuberculosis and other causes.

Symptoms: The patient will have temperature which will rise in the evening along with headache and stiffness. Sometimes the patient may also develop convulsions and unconsciousness. It is always preceded by irritation, sleeplessness and delirium. It may range from 2 days to months. The fever usually disappears with paralysis generally of the lower extremities.

Treatment: It is a contagious disease, so the patient should be isolated.

1. Brihat Vata Chintamani (100 mg.)
   Vata Ganjankusha (100 mg.)
   Pravala Bhasma (Chandra puti) 100 mg.
   } with Amritarishta (1 ounce) twice daily.

2. Ekangaveera Rasa (100 mg)
   Mahalakshmi Vilasa Rasa (100 mg.)
   Punarnava (30 grains). This can be given in divided doses thrice daily along with honey.

External Treatment: Mild massage with Mahamasha Taila and Mahavisha Garbha Taila on the entire body except the head must be given for about half an hour. Triphala can be given as a laxative.

The patient's vomit, urine, faeces and nasal discharge must be collected in an antiseptic container or they should be burnt.

DENGUE FEVER

Dengue fever is called Dandaka Jwara in Ayurveda. It occurs in the tropics and sub-tropics.

Signs and Symptoms: The patient will have fever, associated with pain and swelling in the joints with eruption on the body. There will be a constant sore throat, conjunctivitis and pain in the muscles of the body. The temperature may subside after three days or it may last for a month. Dengue Fever is not at all a fatal disease.

Treatment: Mrutyunjaya Rasa (100 mg.) with Pravala Bhasma (100 mg.), Triphala Churna (5 grains) should be administered twice daily with honey.

Diet: The patient must be kept on a liquid diet till the temperature comes down to normal. Milk and fruit juices are usually advised. Mild laxatives like Triphala and diuretics like Punarnavarishta are usually advised.

DIPHTHERIA

There will be a membrane in the throat along with exudation on the tonsils or at the back of the throat or pharynx. It is called Rohini in Ayurveda.

Causes: It is caused due to the vitiation of kapha especially in autumn and winter and it may occur even in adults, though rarely.

Treatment: Kapha alleviating treatment is usually advised. It may be noted here that the false membrane which is present in the throat will discharge a dangerous toxin. This toxin not only attacks the heart muscle but also the nervous system. In modern medicine Anti-Diphtheric serum is given (ADS) and as a prophylactic DPT (Triple Antigen) is given to children; but in Ayurveda the following line of treatment is adopted: Khatphaladi Churna (half gm.), Shuddha Visha (5 mg.), Kaphantaka Vati (one-fourth tablet), Shringa Bhasma + Pravala Bhasma (50 mg.) Kasturibhairava Rasa (5 mg.)

SAND-FLY FEVER

It is called Maru Makshika Jwara in Ayurveda.It is also called Three Days Fever (Trutiyaka Jwara).

Causes: It is caused by phlebotomous papatasis (sand fly). It is very common in M.P., Western U.P., Delhi and Punjab and a rarity in South India.

Signs and Symptoms: Fever, headache, conjunctivitis and all the signs and symptoms of influenza. The temperature will rise up to 104°F and come down to normal within 3 days. During the temperature the pulse will be thready, weak and irregular.

Treatment: The general line of treatment which is adopted for common fever holds good here also. The following line of treatment can also be given:

Guduchi Satva: 200 mg.
Shringa Bhasma: 100 mg.   } Thrice daily with honey.
Jwarankusha Rasa: 100 mg.

YELLOW FEVER

It is called Peetajwara in Ayurveda.

Causes: It is caused by mosquito. It is very common in Africa, Spain, and other foreign countries. Luckily India is devoid of this disease.

Signs and Symptoms: Temperature associated with jaundice and rigor. The temperature will come down within 4 days but it may occur once again on the 6th day. There will be coating over the tongue associated with constipation.

Treatment: The treatment which is adopted in Vatolbana Sannipata Jwara must be adopted here.

MUMPS

Mumps is a disease caused by a virus according to modern medicine. It is called Karnamoolaka Jwara in Ayurveda. It is also known as Pashana Gardabha. It comes under Kshudra Rogas. It is due to the vitiation of vata and kapha doshas.

Signs and Symptoms: There will be swelling in Hanusandhi, which is stable in nature, associated with less pain. It rarely occurs in adults.

Treatment: (1) Lepa of Chandana should be applied twice daily.

Diet: A liquid diet should be given. The important complication is orchitis or oopharitis, so it should be treated with Chandraprabhavati (100 mg.) with Ashwagandharishta (one-fourth ounce) twice daily for 15 days to one month.

HEAT STROKE AND HEAT-EXHAUSTION

Heat stroke and heat exhaustion are known as Anshughata Sannipata and Anshughata Jwara in Ayurveda.

Heatstroke is very common in North India. Heatstroke occurs after heat exhaustion.The temperature may rise up to 108°F.

Signs and Symptoms: High fever, absence of sweating, rapid pulse, thirst, cramps in the muscles and confusion leading to unconsciousness. The patient may also suffer from dehydration and dysphonia.

Treatment: The patient should be given pitta-alleviating treatment. This means that all cold measures like cold foods, drinks and cold baths must be adopted.

Jeerikadyarishta with Drakshasava and Chadanasava must be administered one teaspoonful each with ice twice daily either with Chandanadi churna (200 mg.) or with Shadangapaniya or Mahaushira Panaka. Sometimes Mritasanjeevani sura (one ounce) with juice of Draksha or sugarcane juice can be given three or four times a day. Hemagarbha Potali Rasa in a dose of 100-200 mg.can be administered twice daily; plenty of fluids with sugar and honey with or without salt can be administered to prevent cramps in the muscles.

Lemon juice with a little quantity of common salt and sugar taken during summer season, will act as a prophylactic measures to sunstroke. One should avoid exposing oneself to the hot sun for long periods to prevent sunstroke.

SMALLPOX AND CHICKENPOX

Smallpox is called Masoorika in Ayurveda. It comes under the group of eruptive fevers. In India it has been completely eradicated.

Causes: The patient will have eruptions more profuse over the face, on the distal end of the elbow and below the knee, axillae will be free from eruption; there will be less on the trunk whereas in case of chickenpox, the rashes will be more on the trunk and axillae and less below the knee, below the elbow and on the face. It can also be differentially diagnosed from measles (Sheetala) where there will be vitiation of tridoshas in the body. The temperature will go up to 104°F. It may also lead to internal haemorrhage and later death.

Treatment: Prophylactic measures such as administration of vaccine should be adopted to prevent it. It is an infectious disease, so fomites, faeces, urine, sputum, nasal discharge and other things must be carefully thrown out or burnt. According to Ayurveda usually a mild laxative should be given. Internally a Pitta and kapha alleviating treatment should be adopted.

Either Eladyarishta or Khadirarishta or Chandanasava and Shadangapaneeya may be given in a suitable dose (½ teapsoonful each). Swarna Maskshika Bhasma (100 mg.) with Pravala Bhasma (Chandraputi) (100 mg.) must be administered with Saribadyarishta (½ ounce) twice daily or the juice of neem leaves: ½ teaspoonful with honey twice daily can be administered. The same type of treatment holds good in chicken-pox also.

External Line of Treatment: With bitter leaves like neem leaves, in the form of a paste must be applied. He may also be given a bath with Panchavalkala and Shadangapaneeya decoction. He should be kept in an isolated place to prevent the spreading of the disease.

MEASLES

Measles is an eruptive disease which is very common in children. It is called 'Romantika' in Ayurveda.

Causes: It is caused by Rubeola.

Signs and Symptoms: Initially the patient will have a running nose, sneezing, coughing and hoarseness of voice, and later on he will have eruptions and fever. First rashes will occur either on the brows, chin, cheek, behind the ears or on the neck. The spots will be red elevations above the surface of the skin and the face will appear to be swollen.

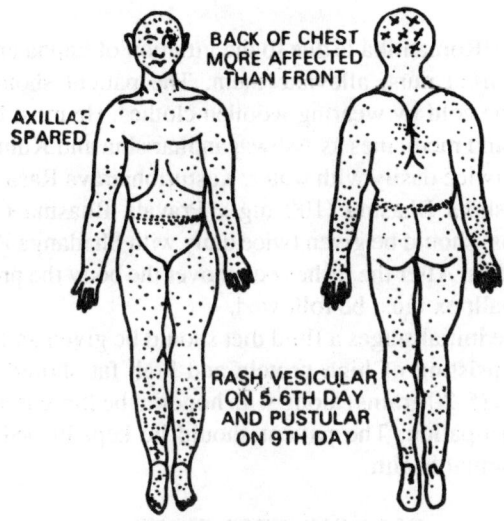

Small-pox

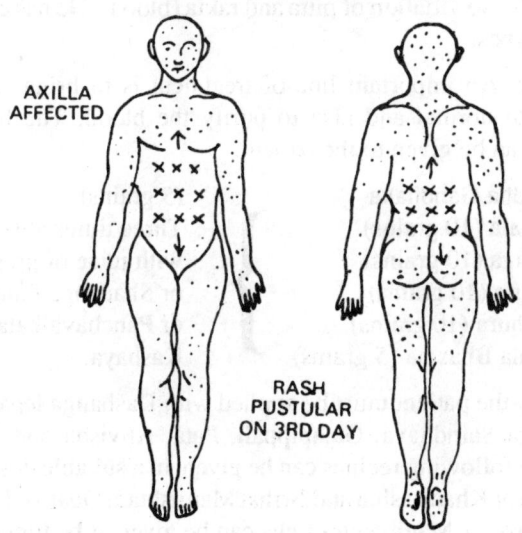

Chicken-pox

Sometimes the rashes may also occur in the mouth and throat, then they fade after 2-3 days. There may be peeling of the skin. In later stages, it may lead on to respiratory complications as broncho-pneumonia and tuberculosis.

Treatment: Romantika is due to the vitiation of kapha and pitta so the medicines used must alleviate them. The patient should protect himself from the cold by wearing woollen clothes. He must he given a nutritious diet and medicines as Ashwagandharishta and Kumari Asava 10 drops each, twice dasily with water. Kasturibhairava Rasa (100 mg.) Swarna Mastashika Bhasma (100 mg.), Pravala Bhasma (100 mg.), Katuki (5 grains) should be given twice daily with Shadanga Paneeya or Dashamoolarishta. After the rashes occur over the body the prescription adopted for smallpox must be followed.

Diet: In the initial stages a fluid diet should be given and later on a normal diet consisting of high protein and high fat should be given. Triphala churna (5-20 grains) along with honey at bedtime is to be given to prevent constipation. The patient should be kept in bed with full physical and mental health.

BULBOUS ERUPTIONS

It is called Visphotaka Jwara in Ayurveda. Sushruta has stated that these eruptions are due to vitiation of pitta and rakta (blood). He has classified this in seven types.

Treatment: An important line of treatment is to bring down the vitiated pitta to normal and also to purify the blood. The following prescriptions can be given to the patient:

1. Shuddha Gandhaka   (5 grains)
    Triphala (10 grains)   Three times a day
    Vidanga (10 grains)   }   with juice of grapes
    Khadira (10 grains)   or Shadanga Paneeya
    Gokshura (10 grains)   or Panchavalkala
    Pravala Bhasma (5 grains)   Kashaya.

Externally the patient must be applied with Dashanga lepa (Vacha, Hingu Vidanga Saindhava, Gajapippali, Pata, Ativisha and Trikatu). Any one of the following recipes can be given in a suitable dose. Either Saribadyasava or Khadirashta and Brihat Manjishtadi Quatha. Laxatives such as Triphala, or Manibhadra Leha can be given at bedtime.

Diet and Regimen: The patient must be given plenty of fluid and gruel till the temperature comes down to normal, and normal diet can be resumed afterwards. He should not be allowed to take hot, pungent things like chillies, spices, curds, and other pitta-provocating foods. He should not be exposed to fire, hot climate and hot sun.

ERYSIPELAS

Causes: It is caused by haemolytic streptococal infection of the skin. It occurs in both sexes at all ages. The eruptions may last for 2-4 days. In Ayurveda it is called Visarpa.

Signs and Symptoms: There will be red patches and an inflamed skin with oedema of the subcutaneous tissue. The edge of the patch is always raised and defined. As soon as the oedema subsides the vesicles and bullae clearly appear on the central part. The face is involved in 80 per cent. The temperature will be usually 104°-105°. If the inflammation is not controlled well in time it will spread throughout the glottis and it may prove to be fatal. This is due to the vitiation of the tridoshas. According to Ayurveda it is of five types. According to Sushruta the type of symptoms, the type of rashes and type of fever will depend upon the vitiation of the doshas involved.

Treatment: The patient suffering from Kaphaja Visarpa must be given an emesis. After emesis he should be given bitter drugs. In pittaja visarpa: blood letting and purgatives are advised. And for producing purgation Triphala decoction has to be given with ghee and Trivrit. For producing emesis the decoction of Patola may be given alongwith Pippali churna and Madana Phala or decoction of Madanaphala, Madhuka, Nimbatwak (neembark). Kutaja fruit can be also given.

External Application: Unguentum prepared out of Rasna, lotus Devadaru, Chandana, Madhuka and Bala must be made into a paste with cow's milk and applied externally. The decoction prepared from Laghu Panchamoola (Gokshura, Brihati, Kantakari, Shaliparni and Prishniparna) with Yava paste must be used internally or externally.

Either Patoladi Kashaya, or Nimbadi Kashaya can be given internally in a dose of one ounce twice daily with an equal quantity of water.

6

GENITO-URINARY SYSTEM
Diseases and Remedies

Introduction: In this chapter we shall consider the diseases of the genito-urinary system, namely, diseases of the kidneys, ureter, bladder, urethra, and the diseases of the reproductive organs.

Diseases of the Urinary-System: In the urinary system, there are two kidneys which are bean-shaped and which are situated in the lumbar region. They are very important organs as their function is to regulate the body constituents—blood filtration and excretion of waste products, and acid-base balance of the body. If they get deranged they will give rise to many complications resulting in renal failure.

Functions of the Kidneys: The important function of the kidneys is to filter the blood to remove toxins and impurities from the blood. The blood passes to the glomeruli and filters the non-protein of the plasma. The remaining portion of the blood then comes back to the heart. The urine will be excreted from the kidneys, through the ureter which opens into the bladder and through the urethra outside. Substances such as sodium, potassium, calcium, magnesium, amino-acids and chlorine are reabsorbed into the system and are thrown out through the urine in the form of phosphates, urea and uric-acids. When the kidney fails to excrete all these things, then toxic materials like uric acid will accumulate in the blood and urea resulting in "Uraemia". The kidney regulates the water and electrolytic content of the body, and maintains the normal acid-base equilibrium of the body and retention of other substances vital to the body economy such as glucose amino-acids, phosphates, bi-carbonates and proteins. Glucose is normally re-absorbed by the system completely by the proximal tubules. The kidney excretes the waste products of metabolism and toxic substances. The end products of metabolism are proteins, urea, uric-acid, creatinine, phosphates and sulphates. It also regulates the hormonal functions of the body. In health and in the temperate climates the urine excretion in 24 hours will be about 800-2500 ml.

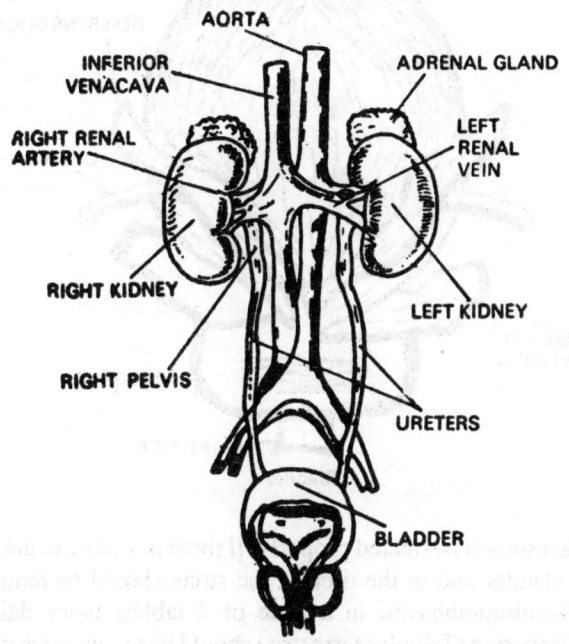

Urinary Tract (Kidneys and Ureters)

DYSURIA

Dysuria refers to difficulty in passing urine due to many causes: they are, spasmodic stricture (Vatakundalika), retention of urine (Vata vasti), distended bladder (Mutra jatara), suppression of urine (Mutrakshaya), enlarged prostate (Mutragranthi), cystitis or urethritis (Ushna vata), scanty urination (Mutrasada), or atonic condition of the bladder (Vasti Kundala). The obstruction of urine may be partial or complete. This may also be due to tabesdorsalis, threadworm, gonorrhoea, urethral stricture, hysteria and hyperacidity of urine.

In Ayurveda it is called Mutrakrichra and is clinically classified into seven types.

Treatment: If it is due to acidity of urine, it should be made alkaline by the use of alkaline drugs like Kshara and diuretics. If it is due to

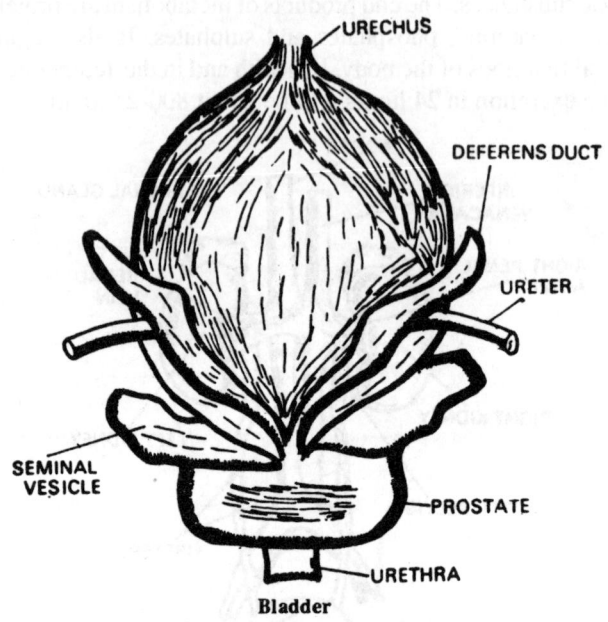

gonorrhoea it should be treated properly. If there is a stone in the kidney, ureter and bladder and in the urethra the stone should be removed by surgery. Chandraprabhavati in a dose of 2 tablets twice daily with Gokshura decoction (Tribules terrestris) should be given in a dose of one ounce either Sarivadyasava or Usheerasava, or Chandanasava either alone or mixed together should be taken in a dose of 1 teaspoonful, twice daily with an equal quantity of water alongwith 2 tablets of Chandanadi vati thrice daily. Trinapanchamoola Kashaya can also be given together with Shilajit in a dose of one ounce with 200-250 mg. twice daily.

HAEMATURIA

The bleeding from the urethra may be due to some of the causes that have been already narrated in dysuria.

Causes: In Ayurveda it is called "Adhogata Rakta Pitta". It is a condition wherein blood will be passed through the urine. The important causes leading to Haematuria will be stones, cystitis and nephritis.

Treatment: `Treat the cause' is the best treatment. Prepare a milk decoction of Shatavati (Asparagus racemosus) and Gokshura (Tribulas

Kumari (Aloevera)

terristris) to be given in a dose of one ounce twice daily with or without Gomutra Shilajit 200 mg. It is an exudate obtained from the rocks having the smell of cow's urine. It is not only effective as a urinary antiseptic but also acts as a rejuvenating drug.

Diet: One should avoid acutely hot, pungent and saline foods. The patient should not expose himself to hot climate and hot things. He is advised to take bittergourd, drumsticks, dadima (pomegranate) and juice obtained from citrus fruits. The patient should be forbidden from sexual intercourse. Meat soups can also be given. The patient is advised to take plenty of fluid, water, sugarcane juice and grape juice.

AMENORRHOEA

It is condition wherein there is an absence of menstrual flow in the females. Menses usually starts at about the age of 12 to 16 years, depending upon the climatic conditions and stops at the age of about 45 to 50 years.

In Ayurveda it is called Nasta Raja, physiological amenorrhoea. It usually occurs at the onset of pregnancy, after menopause and before puberty.

Pathologically it may be due to any pathological lesion in the uterus or anaemia.

Treatment: Amenorrhoea which occurs due to pregnancy need not be treated. In case of menopause the complications arising from it are to be treated.

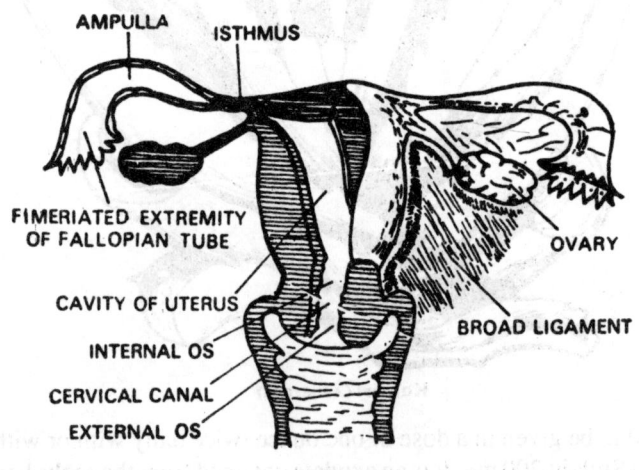

Uterus

Irregular amenorrhoea must be treated suitably. If a lady has reached puberty and does not get menses, then she should take fish, tila (gingelly seeds), Kulattha (horsegram), Masha, sour diet and Madya (alcohol). The Amla diet like Amalak and Dadima etc., and alcohol in suitable quantity, cow's urine, curd diluted with half quantity of water, and Sura (an alcoholic preparation made from roots, fruits, oily substances and salts) should be mixed with food and given to the patient.

Locally: (a) Sweda or fomentation should be made on the lower abdomen after applying castor oil or any other oil, with leaves of Nirgundi (Vertex Nirgundi).

(b) A poultice prepared from the leaves of Eranda (castor) and flowers of Palasha, should be applied on the lower abdomen.

(c) Internal Medication: A juice obtained from Aloe barbedenisis (Gritha Kumari) can be given in a dose of one ounce twice daily for a week. Raja Pravarthini vati should be given in a dose of 2 tablets twice daily with Raja Pravarthakavalehya.

MENORRHAGIA

Menorrhagia is a condition where a woman will notice excessive bleeding during her menstrual period associated with relative symptoms. In Ayurveda it is called either Asrugdhara or Rakthapradara.

Treatment: A ghee prepared from usira should be administered after Panchakarma—Pentad of purification procedures. (Readers are requested to go through *The Panchakarma Treatment of Ayurveda* by the author.)

A decoction prepared from sandalwood (Srigandha) in a dose of half an ounce with half an ounce of Doorva (Cybodondacty lanlinn) along with sugar candy or a ghee prepared from Asanadigana should be given, 2 teaspoons twice daily.

External Treatment: A special type of enema should be administered into the uterine cavity. A douche with Panchavalkala Kwatha should be given twice daily.

Prepared Medicines: Ashokarista one ounce twice daily, or Pradarantaka rasa 2 to 5 grains twice daily with rice water. Pushyanuga churna 1 teaspoonful with Laksha powder 20 grams can be given.

METRORRHAGIA

It is a condition where there will be excessive bleeding from the uterus from the onset of puberty or at any age. In Ayurveda it is included under Adhogata Rakta Pitta (Asrigdhara).

Ashoka (Lat. Saraca Indica)

Treatment: The juice of Ashoka (Saracaosoca dewilde) bark or the juice obtained from the Shatavari root (Aspharagus recemosuswild) with Vasaka 2 teaspoonful each twice daily with Laksha churna in a dose of 10-40 grains must be taken internally.

Doorvadi Ghrita: 1-2 teaspoonful with Pravalapanchamrita 5 grains along with milk or Pushyanga churna—40 grains with 10 grains of Pravala Pisti and 500 mgs. of Chandraprabhavati twice daily. Usheerasava or Ashokarista or Lodhrasava can be given in a dose of 1 ounce with equal quantity of water. The flowers of banana trees should be given along with curds twice daily.

Diet and Regimen: The patient must be told to take complete bed rest. Any physical and mental strains must be avoided, including excitement, anger and worry.

The foot end of the bed is to be raised and the head end should be lowered till the bleeding stops.

Irritants and spicy or pungent foods must be avoided. Grape juice, banana juice and pomegranate juice should be given to the patient.

LEUCORRHOEA

Leucorrhoea refers to a whitish discharge which occurs from the vagina. This may be associated with a viscid, thick and foul smelling discharge.

Causes: The white discharge seen in women who are in the habit of taking heavy, oily and viscid food which aggravates kapha. It may be due to disorders of digestion and sedentary habits.

Symptoms: The woman will complain of a white, offensive dicharge with vomiting, anorexia, chest pain, cough, difficulty in breathing and pruritis.

Internal Treatment: A powder of root of ladiesfinger (Abelmoschus esculantus moench) alongwith Shatavari and Atimadhura and Masha 2 grams (Phaseolusmungolinn) 2 grams should be taken with cow's milk and sugar twice daily.

External Treatment: A douche prepared with Panchavalkala or Triphala, alum, seeds of mango, seeds of jamboo and flowers of dhataki with honey must be given. They are astringent medicines which will stop the Leucorrhoea effectively.

Prepared Medicines: Chandanasava-1 teaspoonful with an equal quantity of Sarivadyarista can be given with Chandraprabhavati, 2 tablets, twice daily. Lukol tablets may be taken in a dose of 2 tablets twice daily or Femiplex tablets (charaka).

Even the juice of either Kumari or bark of Lodhra or Ashoka can be given in the form of decoction one ounce twice daily with an equal quantity of water.

URINARY CALCULI

It is a stone formed in the urinary tract due to the calcium phosphate or oxlates. The stone may be formed either in the kidney, ureter, or

Pashana bhedha

urethra. If it is formed in the kidney and detached into the ureter it causes excruciating pain.

Causes: According to Ayurveda stones are usually formed in the body because of vitiation of vata and kapha. It is clinically classified under four heads, i.e., (1) Due to vata, (2) due to pitta, (3) due to kapha and (4) due to shukra. Kapha plays a prominent part in the production of stones. These stones are called Asmari in Ayurveda.

Signs and Symptoms: The patient will notice pain which will be excruciating. It will be present in the region of the kidney and in the lumbar region. The pain will be radiated towards the genital organs. At times, the patient will have fever, loss of appetite, sleeplessness, painful urination and vomiting. Sometimes he may notice blood in the urine.

Treatment: The decoction of Varuna (Cretiva religiosa) can be given twice daily in a dose of one ounce. The bark of this tree is taken   and boiled with a sufficient quantity of water, reduced to one-fourth its quantity of water to be given twice daily.

Pashana Bheda (Bergenia ligulata) is the drug of choice in the treatment of urinary stones. Usually rhizome of this plant is very beneficial. Sometimes the decoction of Kulattha (Dolichus biflorous) is a very good lithotroptic. Prepared medicine like Chandraprabhavati can be given in a dose of 2 tablets twice daily with one teaspoonful of Shilajit Rock exudation Bitumen in warm milk. Traikantaka Ghritha can be given in a dose half an ounce to one ounce on an empty stomach early in the morning. Coffee prepared from Gokshura should be taken two to three times in a day.

Diet: The patient is advised to take rice with soup of Kulattha. Before and after food Traikantaka Ghritha must be used. He must avoid excess of milk and calcium products in his diet.

SYPHILIS

Causes: It is produced due to sexual contact of a male with an infected female, or otherwise. In Ayurveda, it is called Firanga and it is found in a Sanskrit book on medicine called *Bhavamisra* of the 16th century. Sometimes it is also called Upadamsha. It has three stages: (1) Primary, (2) Secondary and (3) Tertiary stage. Syphilis may be either acquired or inherited. In Ayurveda it is clinically classified into five varieties, namely—due to vata, pitta, kapha, rakta and due to tridoshas.

Symptoms: When a male or female has sexual intercourse, and if there is infection in any one of them, then it will produce the disease called Syphilis. Initially in the male, there will be hardening of the glans penis; if it is neglected it will go into the secondary stage. It is caused by treponema pallidum. In the female, in the initial stages, it will not be noticeable at all. So it passes into the secondary or tertiary stage. In the male chancres heal in about 68 weeks leaving a scar. In the secondary

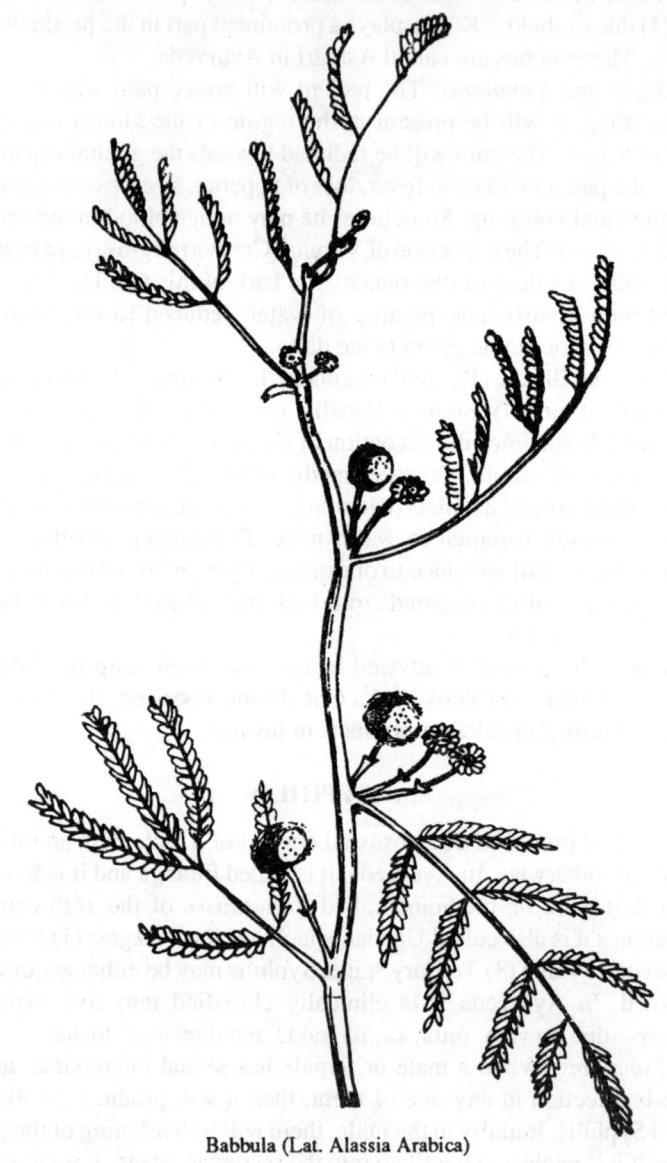

Babbula (Lat. Alassia Arabica)

stage the patient notices an enlargement of the lymphnodes and nephritis, arthritis, condylomata in the anal margin, vulva, under the breasts and in the throat there may be red snail track, alopecia which may be general or local and jaundice. It reaches the tertiary stage with punched out ulcers, swelling in the muscles and bones and it will attack almost all the organs of the body. In case of congenital syphilis the child will die in the womb of the mother, before its birth or due to a miscarriage. The child may be both deformed, deaf or have a depressed nose, etc.

Treatment: The main treatment lies in giving a purgative and a soothing application to the affected parts. Externally, Satyanasi Taila which is prepared from Satyanasi (Argemony medicona) or Koshatakyadi Taila, may be applied. An ointment made out of the juice of apamarga and little opium can be applied to the part affected. Internally, Upadansahara vati should be given in a dose of 2 tablets twice daily. Prepared medicines like Chopachinayda Choorna in a dose of 40 grains twice daily can be taken with Sabira or Sarivadivati, 1 to 2 pills with butter. Saribadyarista with Saribadilehya (one ounce plus one teaspoonful) twice daily should be given. Manikyarasa or Upadansasurya in a dose of 200 mg. with Manjistadi decoction should be administered twice daily.

Diet: Rice, til oil, meat soup, soup prepared from green gram and vegetable soup like bittergourd and milk (may be cow's or goat's) should be taken. The patient should not take buttermilk, jaggery and should avoid sleeping during the day time.

GONORRHOEA

Causes: It is caused by the sexual contact of an infected male with a female or vice versa. It affects the mucus membrane of the urethra in the male and the vagina in the female and later spreads to other parts of the body.

Symptoms: The patient will have a yellowish-white discharge while passing urine, with dull pain. The glands near the organs will be enlarged. If it is not treated at this stage, it may go into the chronic stage producing a lot of complications. It will spread from one person to another via clothes, utensils, etc. It is called Ushana Vata in Ayurveda.

Treatment: Take Bala Menasu 1 teaspoonful and add 1 cup of milk and 3 cups of pure water to it and boil it till it is reduced to 1 cup. It should be taken twice daily with 200 mg. of Gomutra Shilajit; or Pooyamehantakarasa 250 mg. with 500 mg. of Chandanadivati should be given twice daily. The urethra should be irrigated with honey. It will reduce the pain, swelling and it stops pus. Rasmanikya and other prescriptions which have been prescribed for syphilis can also be given.

PUERPERAL FEVER

Causes: It is called Sootika Jwara in Ayurveda. This is caused by untimely delivery, taking of food at irregular times, and too much excitement.

Symptoms: Cutting type of pain in the body, tremor, thirst, heaviness, oedema, pain in the abdomen and loose motions alongwith fever, which usually occurs on the second or third day after the delivery.

It is the most common cause for the death of women after delivery. It is caused by unclean habits which leads to infection. There will be pain in the lumbar region and pelvic region due to inflammation. If it is not treated at this stage, then it may lead on to a stage called Peritonitis (inflammation of the peritoneum). In some of the cases Septicaemia or general blood poisoning may occur alongwith the inflammation of the heart. This condition in Ayurveda is known as Sootika Jwara. In modern medical term it is called Puerperal Fever.

Treatment: Fasting, anointing of the body, sudation therapy, intake of food consisting of bitter, pungent and hot substances, soup prepared from dry raddish and horse gram must be given to vegetarians. For non-vegetatians meat soup should be given. The specific treatment for puerperal fever is to administer a decoction prepared from Dashamoola along with cow's pure ghee. If the pain and fever are associated with kapha dosha, then coriander and dry ginger should be added in a dose of 5 grains each to the above decoction and given in a dose of 1 ounce. Alternatively Dashamoolarista can be given in a dose of one ounce twice daily with an equal quantity of water.

Devadarvyadi Kwatha-2 teaspoons twice daily.

Prophylactic Treatment: The patient is advised to take a decoction prepared from Krishna Jeeraka in a dose of 1 ounce for at least one week. This is in vogue in almost all the houses of Karnataka to prevent the puerperal disease (a teaspoonful in 500 ml. of water reduced to one-fourth).

Prepared Medicines: (1) Pratapalan keshwara rasa 2.5 grains should be given twice daily with Dashamoolarista 1 ounce with an equal quantity of water.

Diet and Regimen: Food which increases appetite like gruel prepared from fried rice, should be given twice daily. Milk can also be given, but it can be administered with 10 grs. of dry ginger. The patient must be given completele rest in bed and her genitalia should be cleaned properly with Dashamoolakwatha or Panchavalakala Kwatha.

DISPLACEMENT OF UTERUS

Causes: Displacement of the uterus takes place when a woman, after delivery, takes heavy food at irregular times, or due to the disorders of food. It is one of the 20 types of Yonivyapatas, according to Ayurvedic Acharyas, such as Charaka. It is produced due to the vitiation of vata, pitta and kapha and tridoshas together; each dosha produces five types of Yonivyapata and remaining five Yonivyapgata are produced by all the three doshas together.

Normally, displacement of the uterus takes place in the case of a woman, who is aged and who has given birth to too many children. It is otherwise called Uterine Prolapse. In this disease, the uterus will slip downwards in between the space of the bladder and the bowel and at times it may protrude from the vagina with offensive smell. This may be due to infection.

Treatment: This condition can be treated either medically or surgically. The surgical line of treatment is the sure and permanent one. However, in the initial stages of the disease, the medical line of treatment still holds good. It should be adopted as follows:

The main treatment lies in treating the predominant vata dosha with oleation; sudation and different types of enemas and later on treating other doshas like pitta with cold irrigation, anointing of the body, and plugging of the vagina with ghee prepared from Jeevaniya Gana; internally also this Ghritha can be given. In case of vitiation of Rakta blood-letting is advisesd. In case of kapha dosha, Vesawara and Krushara (the preparation of rice, til and masha) should be kept inside the vagina for 2 to 3 hours; for this purpose even Bala Taila can be used.

Special Treatment: It is the first duty of the physician to bring the prolapsed uterus to its normal position, by applying ghee over it and irrigating it with luke warm milk and by plugging it heavily with Vesawasra. It should be removed only when the patient has to pass urine.

Diet: A highly nutritious diet should be given and exercises which bring the uterus to its original shape and place must be advised. The patient should be advised to avoid any stress, strains and excessive exertion.

STERILITY

Sterility can be either in males or in the females. In the case of females it is a condition, wherein a lady will be unable to conceive and in the case of males either the failure or incapability to impregnate the female, and these two conditions must be clearly differentiated, that is, either the frigidity or the impotency in the male. Impotency is failure to perform the conjugal union or sex act or to perform it properly. This is especially in the males. Conception is the union of the sperms of the male and the ovum of a female. This union occurs when the sperms are discharged during intercourse from the male genital organ penis into the vagina of the female and there onwards they travel into the uterus, mix with the ovum which is secreted by the ovaries and is detached into the uterus. When this cannot occur, then the woman is considered to be sterile. On the other hand, if a male does not have sufficient number of sperms he is consideried to be sterile. Sterility depends upon several factors which produce diseases and derangement in the organ, which are enunciated in the production of foetus. This is mainly due to the vitiation of tridoshas.

The causes for sterility in the females are important diseases of the fallopian tubes, uterus and ovaries, and hormones which control the functions of these organs. If sterility is due to functional defects of these organs then it can be treated successfully with Ayurvedic treatment. If it is due to structural defects like trauma to the genital organs then sterility must be treated surgically. With regard to females even congenital deformity of the uterus, or any causes producing inflammation of vagina or uterus and displacement of the uterus, will produce sterility in females. Even diseases like anaemia, blood poisoning, and malnutrition may also cause sterility in females.

Treatment: "Phala Gritha" is the famous treatment for curing sterility in females. It should be given in a dose of one ounce with 200 mg. of Vangbhasma twice daily. If there is any suspected defect in the female genitalia, then one teaspoon of the juice obtained from Kshirini should be administered on the fourth, fifth and sixth day of the menses for three months. The plant should be taken along with its roots and cleaned with clean water, then the juice should be obtained and administered in the morning only with milk. It has been tried successfully in our hospital.

Prepared Medicines: Puspadhanva Rasa in a dose of 4 to 5 grains with honey should be given along with warm milk twice daily. Shilajit can be given in a dose of one teaspoonful twice daily and Bala (Sida rhombifolia) can be used internally as well as locally for treating sterility successfully. Externally, it can be used as a douche, to prevent any defects in the genital tract. It can be given internally along with cow's

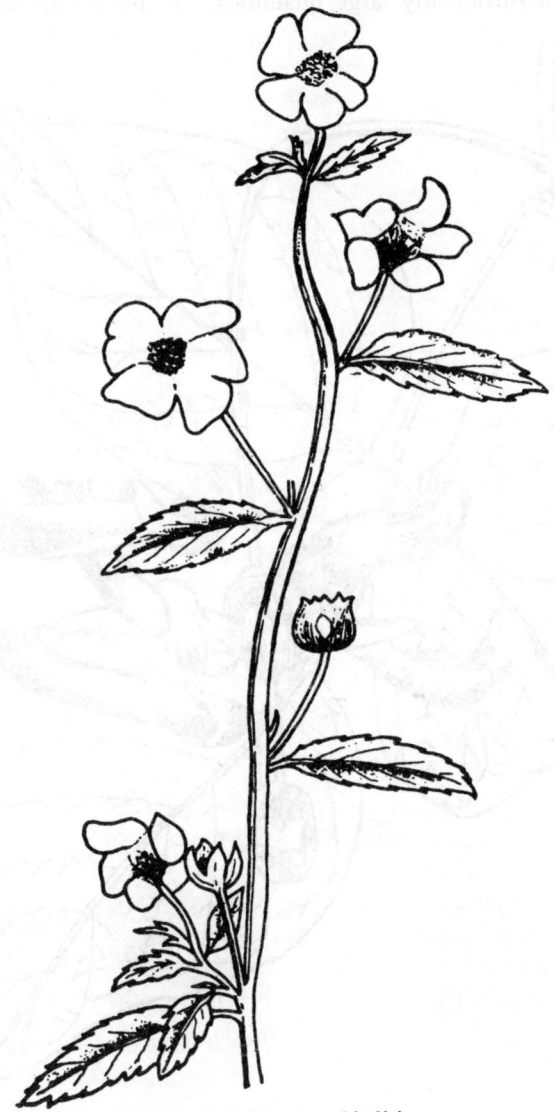

Athibala (Lat. Sida rhombitolia)

milk   in a dose of one teaspoonful once twice a day.

Diet: Food consisting of cow's ghee, cow's milk along with old rice should be given to the patients as also sweet things and fruits must be given in sufficiently large quantities. The patient should avoid hot,

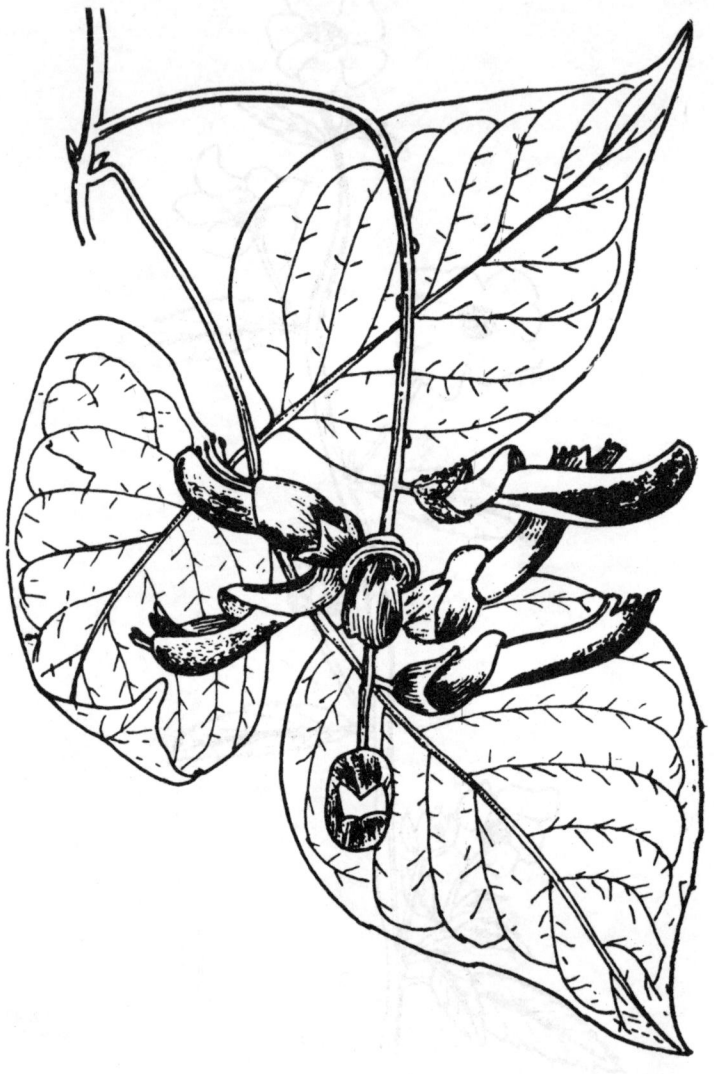

Kapikachu (Lat: Macuna prurensis)

pungent and alkaline foods and too much of fat food, as they have a bad effect on the production of ovum in the female.

Male Sterility: It may be noted here that for the production of offspring, there must be sufficient quantity of sperms secreted by the testes. When there is an absence of sperms in the semen then such a condition is called Azoospermia. When they are in small number it is called Oligospermia. In such cases the conception will not take place. The treatment of a condition like Azoospermia is however difficult to cure but in case of Oligospermia, the treatment according to Ayurveda, is very easy to get a cure. If there are any congenital defects in the testes or in the body of the male, then they must be corrected properly. It should be noted that sterility is different from impotency, the latter being a

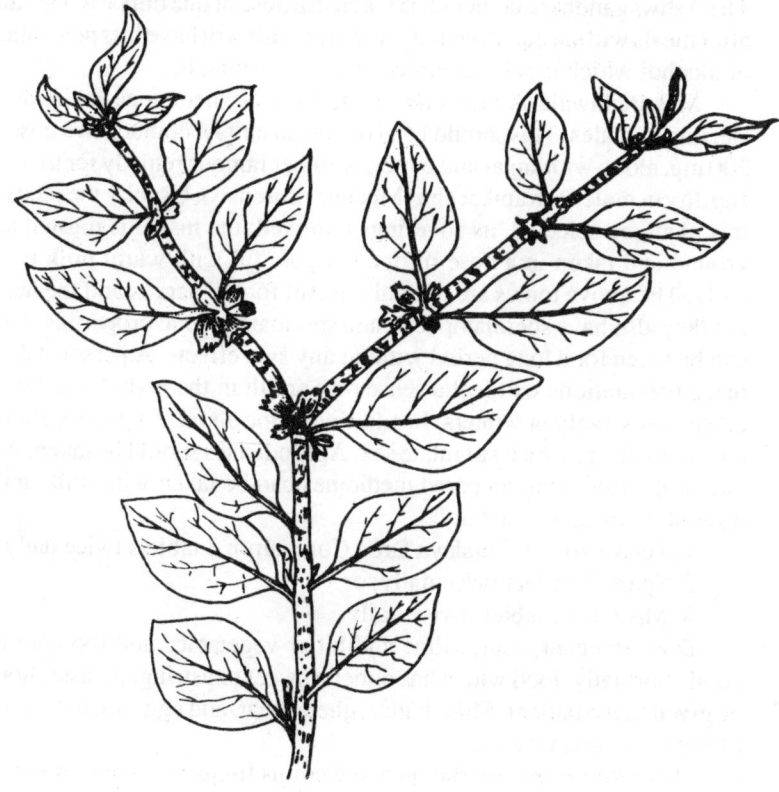

Ashwagandha (Lat. Withania somnifera)

condition wherein the male will be incapable of conducting the sexual act, and as a result the sperms with semen will not be ejected into the female genital tract at all. So, it should be corrected with proper medicines. In Ayurveda, there are some effective medicines for correcting sterility in the male. Ashwagandha (Withania somnifera) is the choice drug for male infertility. The meaning of the word "Ashwagandha" is: "Ashwa" means horse, "Gandha" means smell. The fresh root of this plant has smell of a horse's urine. But the smell disappears after exposing the roots of the plant for some time. This can be taken either in powder form, in the form of a linctus or in the liquid form of Arista after meals. The powder of the dried root can be taken in a dose of one teaspoonful twice daily with milk. So also the linctus can be taken in the same dose. The Ashwagandharista should be taken in a dose of one ounce twice daily after meals with an equal quantity of water. This will have less percentage of alcohol which is self-generated after preserving it.

Makaradhwaja is also one of the famous medicines for treating sterility in males. This should be given on an empty stomach in a dose of 200 mg. along with sugar and butter. Another famous remedy for treating sterility in males is Kapikacchu (Mucuna prurensis). Usually the seeds of this plant are selected, its coverings removed; the inside is roasted and ground and taken in a dose of one teaspoonful with warm milk twice daily. The above tonics are not only useful for the nerves and the heart, but they also have spermatopoetic and spermatogenetic properties. They can be taken for a long period without any side effects. A person taking these preparations will feel a sense of warmth in the body, so it can be taken excessively in winters. In addition to the above drugs, one should take those drugs which stimulate sex. Aphrodisiacs should be taken. Any one of the following prepared medicines can be taken with milk in the dose of 2 tablets twice daily:

1. Tentex forte (Himalaya Drug Company): 2 tablets twice daily or
2. Spark 2 tablets twice daily, or
3. Mustong 2 tablets twice daily.

Diet: Pungent, sour, saline and bitter vegetables and food are not good. Normally food which has either a sweet or astringent taste should be given to the patient. Milk, butter, ghee, meat, and eggs are to be given in excessive quantity.

Other Regimens: He should avoid coitus frequently with his wife. It should be regulated to the minimum in a month.

IMPOTENCY

In Ayurveda impotency is called Klaibya. It may be due to the vitiation of any of the tridoshas of the body.

Causes: Young boys who are in the habit of masturbation and some people who ejaculate at the onset of coitus itself may suffer. Impotency may be real due to either physical or organic causes or according to Charaka and Sushrata it may be due to the perversive sex and over-excitement of the sexual activity.

It may be due to congenital or acquired defects, and it is classified into five types:

1. *Asekyya* is a condition wherein the male is actually excited and stimulated on licking the semen.

2. *Sougandhika* is a condition wherein the male is stimulated and excited as soon as he smells the vagina of the female.

3. *Kumbhika:* It is a condition wherein sexual excitement is noticed in the male only when he conducts a passive sexual act on the anal portion of an individual.

4. *Irshyaka:* It is a condition wherein the person gets sexual stimulation, after seeing the sexual act of others.

5. *Shandaka:* It is a condition wherein an individual has the properties of male but in the sexual act, he behaves like a female.

Treatment: In Ayurveda "Vajeekarana" treatment is of paramount importance in treating impotency successfully. A high protein diet like eggs, fish, testicles of goat, eggs of crocodile, meat of partridge, meat of hen, masha, ghee and butter are very useful.

Internally: Aptyakara Swarasa, Vanari Gutika, Madananda Modaka, Mrut Sanjeevani sura, Makaradhwaja, Chandrodaya Rasa, Veerya Stambhana Vati. *Externally*—Ashwagandha Taila, or Rasa Chandanadi Taila or the Himcolin cream or Lingavardhana Taila are used. Geri Forte: 2 tablets with Tentex forte or Spark (BAN) can be given. The above medicines must be taken after consulting a competent Ayurvedic consultant if they are to be continued for a pretty long time.

Organic impotence resulting from tight foreskin, should be remedied with proper surgery.

7

METABOLISM AND GLANDS
Diseases and Remedies

DIABETES

In Ayurveda Diabetes is called Madhumeha.

Causes: A person who leads a sedentary life and who eats plenty of curd, flesh of goat and sheep, fresh grains and rice, jaggery and all other things which produce kapha (phlegm) in the body will contract Prameha. There are 20 types of Pramehas in the body, which occur due to the vitiation of tridoshas. If they are not treated, they will lead on to Madhumeha or diabetes.

Symptoms: In the early stages of this disease, the patient will notice an excessive quantity of excreta in the teeth, eyes and ears, and he will have a burning sensation in the hands and feet. The patient will also have an oily feeling in the body and will feel thirsty and have sweet taste in the mouth. He will also pass a lot of urine. If the ten types of kaphaja and six types of pittaja are not treated, then they will lead on to four types of vataja pramehas.The Madhumeha may be due to congenital disorders or due to acquqired causes. It is produced due to the loss of tissues, and vitiation of vata. The pitta and kapha may produce obstruction to vata. The urine of such a person will be sweet, just like honey and his whole body will be sweet. He may also develop carbuncles. According to Ayurveda they are 10, and involve the joints, vital organs and muscles tissues. According to the modern system of medicine diabetes is a disorder of metabolism wherein the blood sugar level is increased and as a result one will notice sugar in the urine. There are two types of diabetes: one is Diabetes Mellitus and the other is Diabetes Insipidus. Diabetes mellitus is due to the inaction of the islet of longerhans of pancreas, whereas Diabetes insipidus is due to the non-functioning of Anti-Diuretic Hormone (ADH). There will be excessive quantity of urination with the absence of sugar. In Diabetes Mellitus the patient will pass excessive quantity of urine with sugar and will feel excessive thirst and excessive hunger.

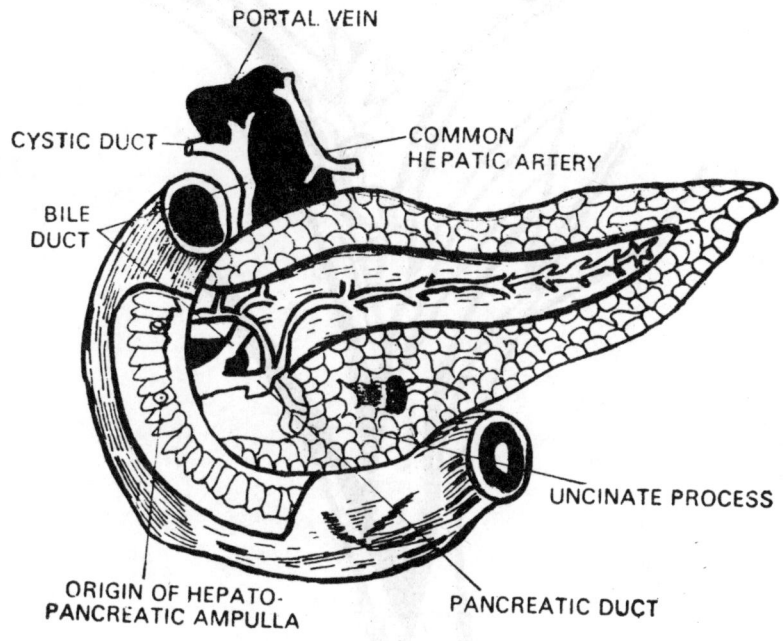

Pancreas and Duodenum

Treatment: One should avoid taking sugar, fats and carbohydrate in one's diet. Sugar containing items like rice, potato, sweet fruits and any sweet preparations must be tabooed. The food should be regulated after examining the sugar in urine (normal blood sugar is 80 to 120mg/100cc of blood) and there will be no sugar in the urine of normal individuals. Fat should be reduced in the diet. The patient should regulate his food habits and should reduce his weight if he is overweight. The juice of Karela (bittergroud) taken in a dose of two teaspoonful twice daily, for 15 days to one month, has brought down the sugar in the blood. The juice obtained from either Bilwa or Neem leaves can also be given successfully. However, bittergourd is the most efficient drug, found to be very effective in controlling the blood sugar. Shilajit (Mineral pitch) is another potent anti-diabetic. Other prescriptions such as Madhunashini, Haridra (Carcuma Longa) and Amalaki (Embica officinalies) are also

Haridra (Lat. Carcuma longa)

famous anti-diabetic agents. A famous Ayurvedic preparation called Vasanta Kusumakara rasa must be administered in a dose of 200 mg. twice daily with sugar or honey, on an empty stomach. A standard prescription is as follows:

Chandraprabha 500 mg., Haridra 500 mg. and Amalaki 500 mg. These should be taken with the juice of Karela (Momardica charantia) twice daily with or without 1 tablet (200 mg.) of Vasanta Kusumakar rasa. D.B.N. tablets of Indian Pharmaceuticals have been found to be effective in reducing blood and urine sugar. Darnisan tablets will also help in reducing the blood sugar.

Diet: It is a rich man's disease. So one should avoid all sweets and its preparations and excessive fat. Instead one should only take bitter vegetables like bittergourd, bimbi and drumstick. Wheat and ragi are very useful.

Other Regimens: A diabetic patient must do those exercises that are fitting to his constitution and strength. He should not sleep during the day. He should avoid injuries as far as possible, as they will not heal quickly and thus produce gangrene, which may require surgical intervention. Yogic exercises, like Matsyendra Asana, Pasthi Mothana Asana and Janu Sheershasana, etc., are found to be very useful in controlling the gravity of the disease to a considerable extent.

OBESITY

Obesity is a condition wherein there is accumulation of excessivie fat in the body. In Ayurveda, this condition is named Medo-Roga. Generally, even in normal individuals, there will be accumulation of fat in the breasts, buttocks and abdomen. An excessive accumulation of fat will also occur in the above places. Man is in the habit of taking fat in oroder to get energy and heat. This will be produced after the fat is metabolised in the body. The fat is obtained from ghee, oils and other fatty substances, which are manily used either as a drink or as a food. It may be noted here thast even nerve fibres contain a fatty material in their convering. The major portion of the brain and also of muscle is derived from fat. Fat is also present in some joints in order to avoid friction and damage to the part at the time of the movement. Whenever we take fat or starchy material in excess they will be deposited in the above mentioned places of the body. The danger of fat accumulation is that it produces cholesterol, which circulates through the bloodstream, in the blood vessels and sometimes it is deposited in the walls of the vessels producing a disease called Hypertension or High Blood Pressure. The liver, kidneys and heart and their functions will also get deranged, thereby leading to many diseases.

Causes: Obesity occurs in a person who is in the habit of not doing any exercise, and who eats too much of food consisting of fatty substances and carbohydrates which produce phlegm in the body, resulting in the production of sweat. Because it contains fat and oily material, the Medo-Roga will be produced.

Symptoms: The person will be unfit to do any work and he has difficulty in breathing on slight exertion, thirst, giddiness, excessive sleep, fatigue in his organs, excessive hunger and at times obstruction to respiration, sweating and an offensive smell from his body.

Treatment: The best treatment for obesity is to perform several exercises. The above person should also avoid sedentary habits, sleeping too much at daytime and eating too much. In Ayurveda, the most famous medicine for curing obesity is a resin, Guggulu (Commiphora mukul). This gum should be purified by boiling it in the decoction of Triphala or cow's urine. It can be given from 10 to 20 grains with a cup of warm milk. Guggulu is present in many preparations, like Triphala Guggulu, Naavaka Guggulu, and can given in a dose of three tablets twice daily.

The famous decoction which has been advocated in Ayurveda for this disease is Varadi Kashaya. This can be given in a dose of 2 teaspoonful twice daily with hot water. In Ayurveda there are Sapta Dhatus with seven types of Agnis or enzymes, which are responsible for digestion, metabolism and nutrition of the tissues. The digestive fire or the Jatharagni is meant for digestion and metabolism of food which includes Medas or fat. So, unless and until these agnis or enzymes are brought into their normal position, obesity will not be cured. Obeynil (Charaka) tablets in a dose of 2 tablets thrice daily with or without Varadi Kwatha will give wonderful results.

Diet: One should avoid sweet and fatty things and carbohydrates in excess. All products which contain a lot of carbohydrates like rice and potato must be avoided. Barley, ragi and maize are the better cereals for the obee. Bitter and pungent things are useful; bittergourd and the bitter variety of drumstick are found to be very useful. The patient may take tea and coffee in good quantities as diuretics. Fruits should be avoided as far as possible and especially those which contain carbohydrate. Chitraka (Plumbago zelyanica) can be given in doses of 10 to 30 grains with honey. Shilajit (5 to 10 grains) with honey and Triphala Kashaya are very effective in reducing fat. Udvartana and body massage are also efficacious in reducing obesity. These massages must be undertaken under the able guidance of a qualified and trained Ayurvedic physician.

GOUT

It is a disease characterised by swelling in one joint, usually the Metatorso Phalangeal joint of the big toe, along with attacks of severe pain. It may spread to the other joints in later course. It is an inborn error of purine metabolism. In Ayurveda it is called Vatarakta.

Causative Factors: The most important cause for gout is the defect in the digestion and metabolism. One should not take food which has contradictory properties. A person who is in the habit of taking excessive salt, sour, pungent, alkaline, fatty and hot substances in the diet and dry food and meat of animals which are reared in watery places, preparations of til (Gingelly seeds), raddish, horse-gram, black gram and curd, alcoholic preparations like Souveera and Shukta, and buttermilk, excitement, sleeping during daytime and eating too much food, a person who is very delicate and living very happily, usually rich people, then in such persons, the Vata and Rakta will be vitiated thus producing Vatarakta.

Signs and Symptoms: The important symptoms of this disease are pain and swelling of the big toe, which will later on spread to other joints of the patient. He will be unable to move and walk without the support of others.

Treatment: The curative line of treatment involves the administration of enema with Gudoochi (Tinosphora cordifolia wild), Ashwatha and Kokilaksha (Asteracantha longifolialinn) along with til oil. It is a disease caused by vata and rakta, so the treatment lies in administering the medicines and food and regimen which eliminate them. The decoction of the root bark of Ashwatha tree (Ficus religious) is very effective. It should be administered in a dose of one ounce twice daily. The oil can also be prepared with the same decoction along with til oil and it can be applied externally.

Panchatiktha Ghritha guggulu should be administered in a dose of two teaspoonful twice daily with hot water or warm milk. It acts as a potent blood purifier. The following prepared medicines can also be given to the patient, either along or together in suitable dosage.

1) Mahamajistadi Quatha -1 ounce twice daily
2) Kaishora Guggulu -2 tablets twice daily

3) Saribadyarista   -1 ounce twice daily
4) Pinda Taila or Gudoochyadi Taila—*For external use* only.

Diet: The patient is advised to take the following diet—old rice, meat soup, wheat, bitter vegetables, garlic and onion.

The following diet should be restricted: fresh rice, curd, fresh wheat and other sour foods and food which is digested slowly.

Other Regimens: The patient should not be allowed any severe exercise nor should he be allowed to sit idle. That is to say, he should move slowly. He should not expose himself either to cold climate, rain or cold baths.

GOITER

It is a disease chracterised by the swelling of the thyroid gland. It is called Galaganda in Ayurveda.

There are several varieties.

Causes: A person who takes food, which causes vitiation of kapha and lessening of pitta is likely to contract Goiter. According to modern medicine, it is due to the deficiency of iodine in the diet. In India and other countries most people living in the hills suffer from this disease.

Signs and Symptoms: The patient notices swelling of the gland in the neck and at times it will be swollen too much, causing difficulty in swallowing and difficulty in respiration.

Treatment: A decoction prepared from Kanchanara (Bauhinavariegata) should be administered in a dose of one ounce along with an equal quantity of water for 10 to 20 days; or the decoction of Varuna (Creataeva neruvala) should be administerd one ounce twice daily with water.

External Use: The leaves of Dhattura macerated with lime and jaggery can be applied over the enlarged gland, or Galaganda Hara Lepa should be applied.

Prepared Medicines: (1) Kanchanara Guggulu-2 tablets twice daily with Aragwadarista or Saribadyarista in a dose of one ounce with water.

Diet: Green gram, Patola, drumstick, bittergourd, old rice, old wheat, milk and its products (except curd). One should not take food which will not be digested quickly and sour. The patient should not take excessive cauliflowers in the food.

Regimen: Those yogic exercises should be performed which activate the thyroid gland to secrete the thyroxine.

8

SKIN AND HAIR
Diseases and Remedies

ECZEMA

It is a skin condition called Pama in Ayurveda.

Causes: One should not take food which has antagonistic properties, excessive fluids, fatty and heavy food and suppressing the natural urges, doing excessive exercise and exposure to hot climate, for with this the vata, pitta and rakta and Kapha are vitiated. The weeping eczema can be correlated to Vicharchika wherein there will be itching, eruptions, oozing and discolouration of the skin.

Treatment: General line of treatment lies in applying only anti-pruritic application of either oil or ointment. Chakramarda Taila or Rasadilepa or seeds of raddish and Bakuchi must be macerated and applied with til oil over the body. After an hour a hot water bath must be given.

Internal Medicines: Blood purifying drugs and food must be administered.

   (1) Mahamajistadi Kashaya -1 ounce twice daily with water.
   (2) Gandhaka Rasayana   -2 tablets twice daily with the abcve Kashaya.
   (3) A laxative which is specifically prescribed for skin diseases, like Manibhadra Lehya should be given in a dose of two teaspoons at bed time.

Prophyllactic Treatment: The patient must be advised strict hygiene by taking baths, wearing clean, dried and ironed clothes to prevent further infections. One should not use the towels, utensils and clothes of the infected persons.

Diet and Regimen: The patient should not take fresh rice, curd, fish, gingily seeds, salt, sour things, milk, jaggery, raddish, and should not indulge in excessive coitus, sleeping during the day and eating too much.

LEUCODERMA

Causes: The causes which have been already mentioned in the production of eczema also hold good for leucoderma. The meaning of the word Leucoderma is white skin. It is due to the lack of melanin pigment in the skin. According to Ayurveda it is called Switra or Kilasa and included in the Kushta. Kushta is nothing but skin diseases including leprosy. However, leucoderma has nothing to do with leprosy. As soon as Switra is produced on the skin of the patient it creates problems for the patient as society will treat the individual with some sort of stigma. It may be even hereditary. The Bhrajaka pitta present in the skin will not function properly: as a result leucoderma will be produced. It is due to the deficient production of pitta. It may be due to even the diseases of the liver.

Signs and Symptoms: The patient complaints of white patch either on the arm or any part of the body kor it may be seen sometimes as raddish-brown small eruptions. There will be a burning sensation, watery exudation and considerable itching. If it involves muscle tissue, then it will become red in colour. Otherwise, if it involves fatty tissue it will be white in colour. It is not curable when the hair inside the patch is white and burnt by fire and also if it is in the joints of the skin and mucus membrane of old individuals.

Treatment: Leucoderma has been traced in individuals who suffer from chronic dysentery. In chronic dysentery there is an impairment of digestion and assimilation of food. The specific treatment for such a disorder is Kutaja (Holarrhena anti-dysentrica). The powder of the bark of this plant must be given in decoction form or as it is. Arogyavardhini vati is also one of the choice drugs for the above disorder. The important composition of this preparation is Katuki (Picrorhiza kurroahoyle). It acts as a stimulant to the liver and thereby helps in curing leucoderma. In the above tablet Tamra Bhasma (copper) is also present which not only helps in the metabolism but also aids in the synthesis of melanin pigment. Another preparation which is commonly used is Bhallataka (Semicarpus anacordium) in the form of linctus. It should be given in a dose of 1-2 teaspoonful twice daily. It may produce a burning sensation in the mouth which can be preventred by applying ghee to the mucous membrane pri to its administration. If any skin eruptions occur due to its administration usually ghee or the pulp of raw coconut will prevent the toxic effects of the drug.

Internal Medicines: Khadira (Accasiacatechu) and Amalaka (Embrlia Officinalis) and Bakuchi can also be given orally.

External Applications: It has been found that the application of Bakuchi (Psoralea corylifolia) along with the seeds of raddish (Raphanus sativuslinn) will cure the disease. These two drugs are to be macerated and mixed with either water or cow's urine and should be applied externally; or Switraghnavati can also be applied externally with cow's urine or Shweta Gunjadi Taila which is prepared from Gunja (Abrus precatorious) may also be applied.

Diet: The patient is advised to take a salt-free and pungent-free diet. Bitter vegetables like bittergourd, are advised internally. Old rice with soup of bitter vegetables or with cow's milk can be given to the patient.

Regimen: The patient must be consoled and convinced that it will be cured and he must be told to avoid anxiety, excitement, emotion, worry and other types of mental strain. He should be informed not to expose himself either to heat or to the sun for a long time. He should not sleep at daytime or stay awake at night. He should also pray to God daily as this will keep him in peace.

PSORIASIS

It is a skin disorder with silvery-grey scaling papules involving papulo-squamous of the skin. It is known as Ekakushta in Ayurveda.

Causes: The disease is caused due to impurities of the blood associated with psychic causes.

Signs and Symptoms: Scaly, silvery-grey papules appear on the exterior surface of either the elbows or knees, or both. Sometimes it will spread all over the body. Psoriasis must be differentiated from syphillitic rashes occurring on the body. The patient suffering from Psoriasis will have patches with violent itching and burning sensation with watery discharge and blood.

Treatnment and Internal Medicines: The patient must be oleated with Pancha Tikta Ghrita Guggulu. It should be administered in a dose of two teaspoonful twice daily with warm milk or warm water. The ghee will regulate the digestion and bowels and stimulate the liver. It will also purify the blood. Manjistadi decoction (Rubia cordifolia) is found to be very useful and it should be administered in a dose of 1 ounce along with an equal quantity of water. Rasamanikya in a dose of 200 mgs. twice daily with honey should be administered with the above decoction.

External Application and Unguentum: The patient'sbody must be subjected to unctuous therapy with Kushta Rakshasa Taila. It should be applied over the body on the patches. It should be removed by taking hot water baths. Green gram powder must be used instead of soap.

Seka and Sarvanga dhara: It is a method of pouring medicaated tailas like Eladi Taila over the body for one hour to one and a half hours for a period of 7-14 days. The patient must be subjected to a hot water bath which is medicated with the drugs that are used in Manjistadi Quatha.

Diet: Pungent, salty and spicy food materials must be avoided totally. Curds should not be eaten. If salt is to be used only rock salt in a very small quantity should be used. All vegetables which have bitter taste like bitter variety of drumstick, bittergourd and Brahmi (Ecliptus alba) are advised.

Regimen: The patient is advised to wear only cotton clothes and not wear any synthetic fibre. It is an infectious disease, so, one should avoid eating food with the patient or using the utensils or clothes of the infected person.

URTICARIA

It is a skin disorder characterised by elevated reddish or pale patches on the skin associated with itching and pain. In Ayurveda this is termed as Sheeta Pitta.

Causes: Exposure to cold air, taking baths in cold waster, psychic causes, and intestinal worms are said to produce this disease. This is nothing but an allergic manifestation occurring on the skin.

Signs and Symptoms: Before the reddish patches appear on the body the patient will experience thirst, tastelessness, heaviness in the body and redness in the eyes. Afterwards, there will be severe itching and pain with or without vomiting. Usually, it occurs in the cold season after an attack of cold. In some of the eruptions there will be redness with elevated edges and depression in the centre. This may also occur due to digestive disorders.

Treatment: Prophylactic treatment lies in using an extra quantity of Haridra (Carcuma longa) in the food preparations. It is used daily by Indians in cooking. If Haridra is to be administered in the form of a powder then it should be taken with milk, sugar and honey. Prepared medicines like Arogyavardhini Rasa, Suthashekara Rasa, Kamadhugarasa can be given in a dose of 5-10 grains daily with honey. The patient's bowels must be made clear with the administration of Triphala tablets 30 gms at bed time. If there are any intestinal worms they must be treated properly. Taking only fresh buttermilk as diet for one to three days, without any medicines, will cure the urticaria.

Unguentum: Eladi (Elettaria carda momum) or mustard (Brassicanigra) oil can be used for external application.

Diet: The patient must avoid sour, salt and pungent food. Curds should be prohibited. All bitter vegetables should be eaten. Plenty of buttermilk which is fresh is advisable.

Other Regimens: The patient's body must be applied with mustard oil along with rock salt and exposed to the sun for some time only and he should not be exposed to cold air. Hot water bath is advised to remove the oil from the body. It is better to use green gram powder instead of soaps to remove the oil from the body.

GREYING OF HAIR

Generally hair becomes grey as a sign of old age. Sometimes the greying process starts at a very young age. This is due to a disease. According to Ayurveda, this is called Palitya.

Psychological causes: Like excitement, anger, passion and mental strain and mostly persons who are of Pittaja Prakriti (constitution) are prone to this disorder.

Other Causes: People who suffer from chronic sinusitis and chronic cold are also liable to contract this disease. It is noticed in some people that even washing of hair with warm water can also lead to early greying.

Treatment: The famous remedy for this disorder is administering Bhringaraja (Eclipta alba) and Amalaki (Emblica officinalis) either in the form of oil or internally. These two drugs should be taken in a powder form in a dose of one teaspoonful each twice daily with milk or ghee. The patient is advised to take plenty of milk and its products. Prepared medicines like Nasrasimha Rasayana can be administered in a dose of one teaspoonful twice daily with milk.

The juice obtained from the leaves of Bilva (Aeglemarwelos corr) can also be applied externally. An application of the leaves of white gunja with Bhringaraja (Eclipta alba) will produce the same effect.

Diet: The patient should avoid pungent, sour things like curds, and spicy food. Instead he should take only milk, ghee, and rice in plenty according to his digestive capacity.

Other Regimens: Hot water should never be used for washing hair and only cold water should be used for bathing. The patient must avoid anxiety, hurry, worry and excitement. If he suffers from a chronic cold and sinusitis then these must be treated properly.

RINGWORM

Ringworm is caused by a fungal infection and is contagious in nature. In Ayaurveda it is called Dadru.

Signs and Symptoms: The patient will notice circular scaly patches with severe itching over the affected parts.

Treatment: An ointment, which is prepared from Cassia, angustifola, macerated with lemon juice, must be applied over the affected part.

Even the oil of lemon grass mixed with coconut oil or til oil will produce the same effect. Dadruhara Lepa or Dadru Damana Malahara or Dadrughnaavati can be applied externally. Internally blood purifying agents and antipruritic agents like Manjistadi decoction, Arogyavardhini tablets and Allerin tablets etc. (2 tablets twice daily) can be administered.

RINGWORM OF THE SCALP

The powder of the seeds of Parijataka (Myctinthis arboristritis) must be applied in the form of an ointment over the affected part. Somaraji taila can also be applied. Internally Saribadyarista can be given in a dose of 2 teaspoons with an equal quantity of water along with purified sulphur as Gandhaka, 1 tablet twice daily. Hot and pungent food is totally forbidden. Only a diet consisting of milk and rice is advised.

DANDRUFF

It is a kind of Dermatitis, mostly found o n the scalp. A typical thin mica-like, scaling on scratching with acute burning and itching sensation will be noticed. Rough papules are seen with itching, without any discharge.

Treatment: An oil prepared from Dhattura leave's or seeds should be applied on the patient's head. Dhattura leaves or seeds are available in the market in the name of Durdur Patradi Taila (Arya Vaidya Shala, Kottakal). It is a dangerous drug if taken internally as it produces symptoms similar to Belladonna poisoning. It should be kept away from

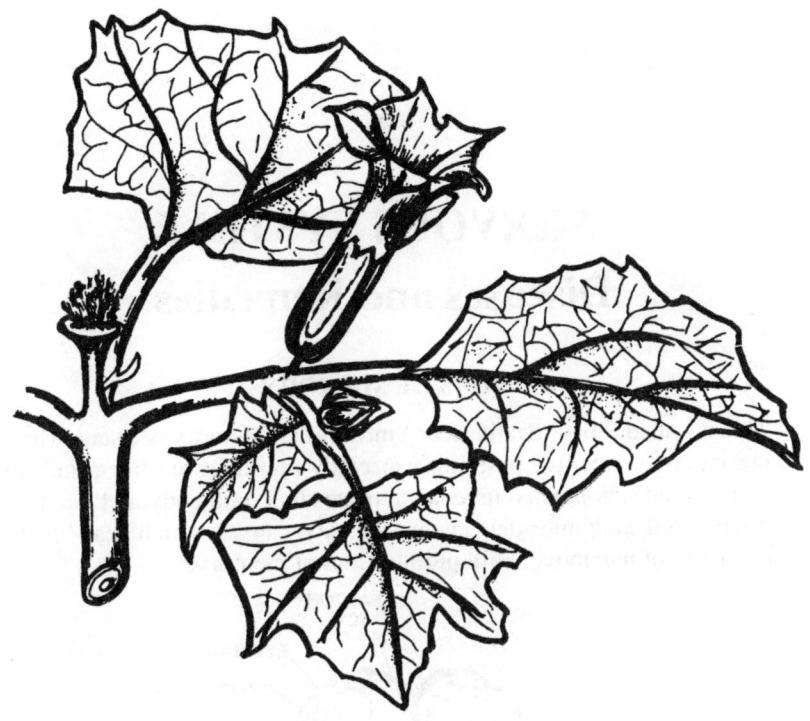

Dhattura (Lat. Dattura Mebal)

children. It can be prepared at home, in the following way 10-12 leaves (1 part) of Dhasttura plant are cleaned and macerated and a decoction is prepared with 16 parts (1000 ml.) reduced to ¼th (250 ml.) of water and to this add til oil or coconut oil 63 ml. and heated on a low fire. It should be taken when only the oil is left (63 ml).

9

NERVOUS SYSTEM
Diseases and Remedies

LOSS OF MEMORY

This is called Smriti Brahmsa or Smritinasha. Memory is a state where one can remember the past. It is especially useful for teachers, students and learned scholars. Ayurveda advocates that both body and mind are interrelated and inter-dependent. So, any causes which lead to the disorders of the above, will produce loss of memory.

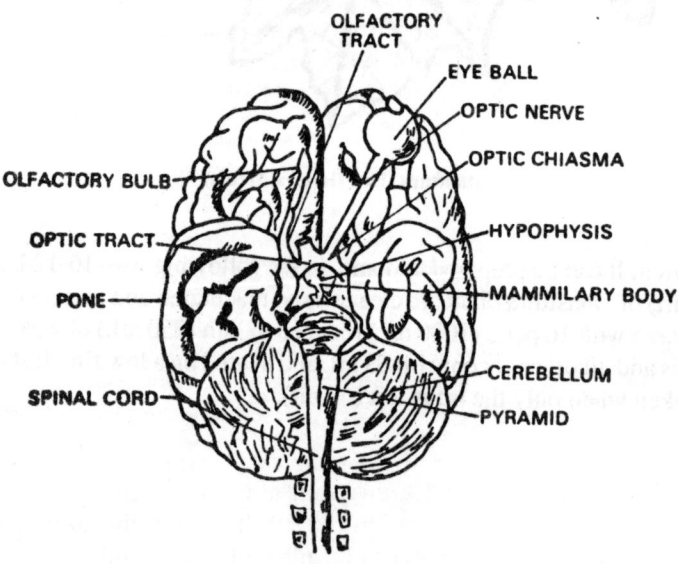

Base (Inferior Surface of the Brain)

Treatment: The best treatment in Ayurveda is to administer pure cow's ghee at least for 15 days to one month with milk. However, drugs like Brahmi, Shankapuspi (Lat. Clitoriaternatoalinn) and Vacha also can be given in a dose of 5 to 10 grains with pure ghee and honey. Brahmi Gritha which is prepared with Brahmi should be given in a dose of 2 teaspoons at bed time only, as also Saraswatha Churna, one-fourth tola (teaspoonful) can be given with milk.

Diet: Cow's milk and cow's ghee are the known remedies. Food which consists of sweets and unctuous are prescribed. The following type of diet is restricted or tabooed—chillies, pungent, bitter and astringent taste is contraindicated.

Amalaki can be given in any form, either in the form of pickles, vegetables, linctus or syrup.

Other Regimens: The medicines which are recommended above will keep the mind tranquil. So, one should avoid excitement, emotion, anxiety, stress and strain. The patients are advised to practical meditation and Yoga, which will promote and correct the memory.

HYSTERIA

Causes: Excessive thinking, sorrow and other mental and uterine disorders produce hysteria. It is a kind of neurosis produced by mental conflict and other mental derangements. It is called Yoshaspasmara in Ayurveda.

Signs and Symptoms: Hysteria occurs only when the patient is awake and it never occurs when he is alone. The eyes and neck will not be deformed, and the patient will not injure either the tongue or any part of the body. The patient will never pass urine and faeces without her control. The muscles and tendons will retain their strength. Hysteria is a condition to the uterus.

Treatment: The patient must be consoled, that is, psychotherapy is the best line of treatment. The patient should be administered an oily enema to make her bowels move freely. 250 ml. of warm gingelly oil can be given as enema.

Nasya: A paste made out of the leaves of custard apple tree, applied to the nostrils will produce immediate relief. It is a vata disorder, hence a vata alleviating treatment should be adopted. The convulsive type of hysteria must be treated properly with Nasya and other vata alleviating treatment. At times the patient starts laughing and weeping with a little excitement. She may be semi-conscious or unconscious with hysterical fits, with paralysis. These conditions do not require much treatment except the line of treatment already explained. Vatakuantaka Rasa, or Vatavidhwamsini Rasa may be administered in a dose of 400 mg. with honey.

EPILEPSY

Epilepsy is a paroxysmal disorder produced due to the disorder of cerebral function with clouding of consciousness with or without localised or generalised convulsions.

Causes: Excessive thinking or any mental weakness will produce this disease and the patient will lose his memory after the attack of this disease. It is called Apasmara in Ayurveda.

Signs and Symptoms: It is of 4 types, namely, due to vata, pitta, kapha, tridoshaja. It occurs once in 12 days and in a month due to the vitiation of pitta, vata and kapha respectively. The patient will have this disease, when he is alone or when he is asleep or it may occur in the company of his friends. The patient will have deformed eyes and neck and will have injury over his organs and tongue. He will pass urine and faeces without his control at the time of convulsions, and there will be contractions of muscles and ligaments. It is not related to the uterus and the patient will go into the stage of sleep after the attack and will have excessive salivation and foam in the mouth. The patient's body will be hot to touch and his organs will be active.

Treatment: The main line of treatment lies in administering errhine treatment to make the patient recover from the attack. The urine of a black cow should be instilled into each nostril, in a dose of 5-6 drops. Brahmi Swarasa can also be given orally, in a dose of one ounce with 1 cup of milk twice daily. The powder of Vacha (sweet variety) should be given in a dose of 30-40 grs. twice daily with honey. The following prescription can be given to an epilepsy patient.

Panchagavya Ghrita-2 teaspoons at bedtime along with milk.

Apasmarantaka rasa: 2-5 grs. with honey twice daily. Smriti Sagara Rasa, Abhraka Bhasma 200 mg. each twice daily Saraswatarishta can also be given 200 mg. with honey ½ oz. with equal quantity of water twice daily.

Siledin (Alarsin, Bombay) tablets containing Chandrika (Sarpagandha) 200 mg., Shankha Puspi (Evolusalsivoides) 67 mg., Bhringaraj (Ecliptalba) 50.25mg., Brahmi (Monniera cuneifolia) 33.05 mg., Jeevanti (Leptadevia

Vacha (Lat. Acorus calamus)

reticulata) 33.05 mg. and Ugragandha (Acorus calamus) 16.75 mg. can be given to Epilepsy patients. Each tablet of Sileden will have the above composition asnd it should be used in 400 mg. strength of 2 tablets twice daily or 3 tablets twice daily for 15 days and continued up to 2 months or more. The dose can be increased or decreased depending upon the condition of the patient or Alert (Vasu pharmaceuticals) can be given in a dose 2-3 capsules twice daily.

SCIATICA

Pain produced due to the sciastic nerve. The pain will radiate from the buttocks, back or the thigh and the leg. It is called Grudhrasi in Ayurveda.

Causes: It is due to the inflammation of the sciastic nerve especially at the region of the hip bone. This is mainly caused by the vitiation of vata and associated with phlegm. Sometimes even physical and mental strain may lead to this disease.

Signs and Symptoms: Initially the patient will experience pain in the lumbo-sacral region which will gradually shift to the back, thigh and leg.

In case of pure vataja type the patient notices above type of pain which is pricking in nature. The patient also notices tremors and

Nirgundi

deformity in the body. In case of Sciatica due to vata and kapha in addition to the above symptoms the patient will have heaviness, tastelessness and excessive sleep and salivation in the mouth. This is according to Charaka. Sushruta has given precise details regarding Sciatica. According to him, the nerve to the thigh and back of the leg will be affected by the vata.

Treatment: Eranda (Ricinus communis) is a famous drug for the treatment of sciatica.This can be prepared in the form of linctus called Erandapaka. One to two teaspoons of this can be given with milk or warm waster. It is a powerful laxative and beneficial to constipated patients. Castor oil can also be given in the form of enema along with Ashwagandha, Bala Bilwa, Dashamoola and water.

The Kshirapaka can be prepared by taking good quality Eranda seeds. Usually 10 seeds are taken, their outer covers are peeled off and a paste is prepared with milk and boiling with a little quantity of sugar. Internally Rasna decoction or Nirgundi with 5-10 grains of Guggulu (old variety) must be administered with one ounce twice daily. Externally the paste made up of Gunja, can be applied with hot water on the painful part.

Saindhvadi Taila is found to be very effective, on applying it with a mild massage in the affected painful parts, i.e., from the buttocks to the leg downwards. Pinda Sweda with rock salt can be used for fomentation in the painful regions. Yogaraja Guggulu 1-2 tablets with Rasna Sapataka decoction can also be given. Vatagajankusha and Sameerapannaga also be advised in this case.

Diet: All fried things, chillieis, tamarind and curds are strictly prohibited. Meat soup prepared from goat, chicken, sheep, and for vegetarians the soup prepared from Masha and Kulattha are advised.

Other Regimens: Excessive rubbing and excessive exercise are strictly prohibited. Cold bath and walking in cold climate are all prohibited.

INSOMNIA

Insomnia is also called sleeplessness. It may be due to mental or physical distrubances. Generally children and people suffering from chronic diseases require more sleep. Physical and mental strain, will lead to sleeplessness. According to Ayurveda this is produced due to the vitiation of Vata and Pitta in the body. Pungent food land exercise immediately after meals, exposure to cold climates, heat, rain or excessive noise may lead to this malady. Sometimes heart disease, high blood pressure, kidney diseases and liver disorders produce severe pain in the body land thereby produce sleeplessness. It may be either temporary or prolonged. It may produce mental and physical weakness associated with indigestion, constipation and flatulence.

Treatment: One should avoid the causative factors that are mentioned above. The Majja of the Vibheetaki (Terminalia-belerica) seeds can be given at bedtime along with milk or Vacha. Amalaki and Brahmi can also be given in a dose of 30 grains, thrice daily along with buffalo milk.

The leaves of Neem (Azadirachta indica juss) macerated with milk and applied to the sole of the foot will produce immediate sleep. Two spoons of til with one cup of warm milk should be administered at bedtime. Even the root of Brahmi Centellaraseiatica urban) prepared in the form of paste and applied on the vertex of the head will produce sleep.

Shirovasthi: A method of keeping oil on the head for about an hour in a leather cap mainly prepared for the purpose. Taila prepared from Karpasa (cotton seeds) can also be used for this purpose.

Dhara: A special type of treatment where medicated buttermilk is constantly and continuously poured over the forehead for one to one and half hour for seven to fourteen days will help cure this disease. Two grams of Amalaki powder is boiled with about two and a half litres of baffalo milk and heated, then a little curd is added and kept at night. In the morning it is churned and the defatted fluid is used for the purpose of dhara.

Diet: One should avoid coffee, tea, smoking cigarette and beedi. One should also avoid seeing films and dramas, constipation and deep thinking. Hot foods are not good for this disease. The patient is advised a diet of rice, green gram, and Amalaki, cow's or buffalo milk, ghee, draksha, Bhringaraja, Patola, and sugar.

Other Regimens: One should avoid thinking too much. Regular massage and hot water baths are very beneficial. Morning or evening walk is also good.

SCHIZOPHRENIA

Schizophrenia is a chronic mental disorder. It is characterised by hallucinations in the form of threatening or unfriendly voices, and with bizarre delusions. It is called Unmada in Ayurveda.

Causative Factors: Stress and strain due to either excessive happiness or excessive fear. Irregularity in the intake of food also plays a very important part in the production of this disease.

Signs and Symptoms: The signs and symptoms of schizophrenia vary from person to person. Generally a schizophrenic patient will lose control of his mind, will have fluctuating moods, a fear complex, timidity, irrelevant speech and loss of power of thinking. He may at times sleep and sometimes act with violent or threatening gestures towards his neighbours. He will not get proper sleep.

Treatment: The important line of treatment is to adopt Dhara over his head and body. This can be done on the head with medicated oils. Ksheerabala Taila is the most commonly used oil for conducting Dhara. The method is very simple. The patient is made to lie on a Droni (log of wood) and the oil which is contained in either an earthen pot or steel vessel is poured on the forehead (in between the two eyebrows) from a distance of about 4 inches. It should be done once a day and with this the patient will get good sleep and will also recover from this disease. Internally vacha (Acorus calamus), Sarpa Gandha (Rouwolfia serpentinja) and Jatamamsi (Nardosta chys jatamasi) are to be given in a dose of 1 teaspoon each twice daily with either milk or cold water; Orsiledin 2 tablets can be given twice daily with milk. Mahakalyana Gritha can also be given in a dose of 2 teaspoons with milk at bedtime. All the above medicines will keep the mind tranquil. Sehdin of Alarsin can be given (2 tablets thrice daily) with milk, and the dose of tablets must be adjusted according to the condition of the patient. Even Vata Kulantaka Rasa, a preparation of mercury can be administered in a dose of one tablet thrice daily with pure honey. Alert capsules can be given in a dose of 2-3 capsules twice daily, or Siledin tablets 2-3 tablets twice daily.

Diet: All types of pulses, beans, fried foods must not be consumed. Astringent and pungent kinds of foods must be avoided. The patient must be told to have milk and its derivatives like butter and ghee in large quantity. Saffron is also found to be useful.

Other Regimens: Schizophrenia is a disease usually arising due to psychic causes. Therefore the patient must be advised and if necessary, induced to pray to God and perform other religious rites. The best thing would be to try to make the patient adopt meditation. It keeps the mind tranquil. All psychological stress as well as strain must be totally avoided and remedied.

10

EYE, EAR, NOSE AND THROAT
Diseases and Remedies

CONJUNCTIVITIS

There will be inflammation of the conunctiva of the eye. It is called Abhishyanda in Ayurveda.

Causes: When a person takes a bath in cold water after exposure to hot sunlight for a long time, seeing things or distant objects constantly, and exposing the eyes to dust and fumes, suppressing the urge of vomiting, eating a light meal at night and suppressing urine, faeces and urges of vata, constant weeping, excessive thinking and other mental causes, excessive coitus and seeing very minute things for a long time will produce eye diseases.

Types: There are 4 types of conjunctivitis viz., vataja, pittaja, kaphaja and raktaja.

Signs and Symptoms: There will be running in the eyes and reddening of eyes with severe pain.

Treatment: Ajanta (Collyrium) is prepared from the roots of Daru Haridra (Berberies asiatica) by boiling 2 tolas of the root with 26 ounces of water, then reduced to 3 ounces and applied with honey to the eyes.

Netra Bindu: A famous eyedrop. It will remove the redness and it cures the pain. Narikelanjana can also be used. Narikela is coconut. Triphala Ghurita: A dose of 2 teaspoons at bedtime along with milk.

CATARACT

Opacity of the lens, which interferes with the vision of the eye is termed as Cataract. In Ayurveda it is called either Timira or Linganasha. The vitiated vata is responsible for this disorder.

Causes: The same causes which are already mentioned in Netra Abhishyanda hold good here.

Signs and Symptoms: When the cataract occurs in the first patala, then the patient will have blurred vision. It may be noted here that the vision has got 4 patalas. In the first stage the whole lens will not be affected and hence the blurred vision occurs.

In case of cataract due to aggravated vata, he will see things which are moving, dusty, reddish and irregular.

In case of cataract due to aggravated pitta, the patient will see the shapes of the sun, vibgyor of the rainbow, and the dancing of a peacock.

In case of cataract due to aggravated kapha, the patient will see things which are white, oily, big and a cloudy sky and sometimes things will be seen drowned and stable in water.

In case of cataract due to aggravated rakta the patient will see things which are red.

In case of cataract due to the vitiation of tridhoshas, he will see different things of different colours and shapes.

Treatment: The main treatment lies in alleviating the vitiated vata. Internally Maha Triphala Ghrita in a dose of 2 teaspoons can be given along with milk at bedtime. It may be noted here that Triphala consists of Hareetaki, Vibhitaki and Amalaki (Terminalia chebula, Terminalia balerica and Emblica officinalis respectively).

If the cataract is in the first or second stage, then medicated ghee will correct the defect, if it is in the third or fourth stage the above Ghrita can be given internally for a period of one month. The juice extracted from drumstick (Morniga pterygosperma gaetryn) leaves (Shigru) along with honey must be applied to the eyes early in the morning everyday. The leaves of drumstick contain a sufficient quantity of Vitamin A. This disease can be prevented by taking the powder of Triphala, about 1 teaspoonful with honey and cow's ghee.

Diet: Cow's milk, cow's butter and ghee are very useful. The following diet can be prescribed to the patient: Rice, wheat, green gram, Patola (Trichos santhes dioica) and drumstick (Morniga pterygosperma), oranges, apples, grapes, banana, and ladiesfingers. Prophylactically drumstick leaves can be prescribed to people to prevent cataract and eye diseases.

Food consisting of sour, bitter, saline and pungent tastes should be forbidden.

Other Regimens: One should not expose oneself excessively either to sun or heat and should also avoid mental excitement, hurry and worry.

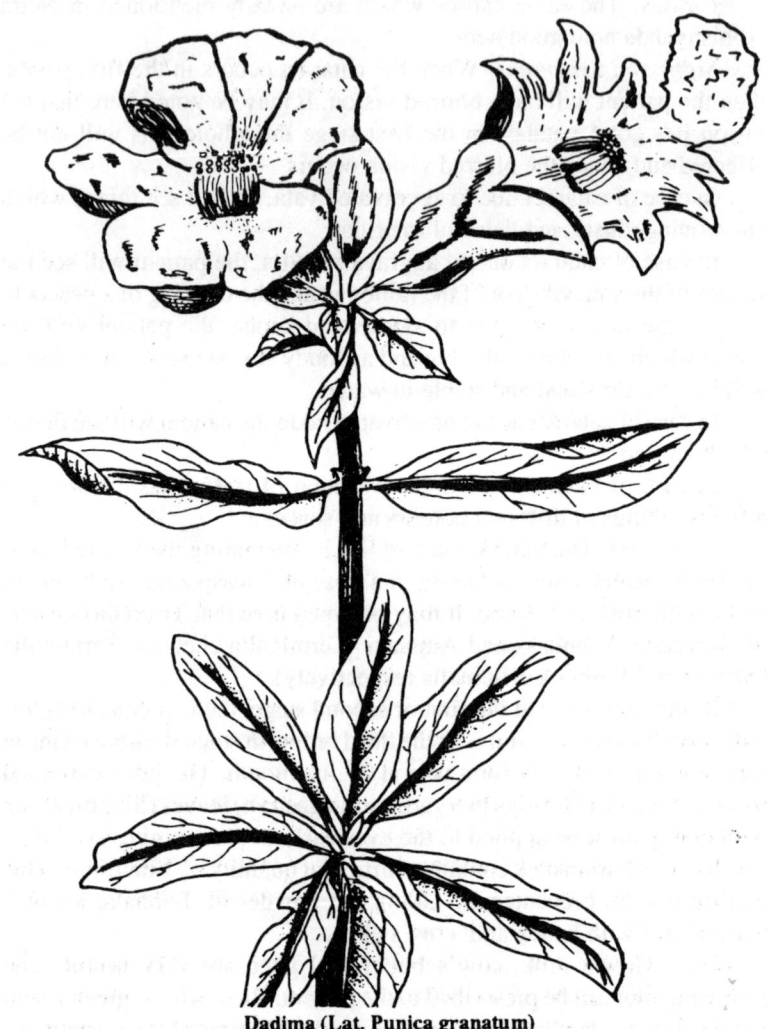

Dadima (Lat. Punica granatum)

EPISTAXIS

Epistaxis is called bleeding from the nose. It comes under Urdhwaga
Rakta Pitta in Ayurveda.

Causes: When a person exposes himself to excessive sunlight, and
does excessive exercise, thinks too much and takes foods having the

following properties. excessively, pungent, sour, saltish, alkaline, the vitiation of pitta and rakta will take place. At times, even high blood pressure may precipitate an attack.

Signs and Symptoms: There will be bleeding from the nose and this must be stopped immediately.

Treatment: The juice extracted from the young flower of Dadima (Punicagranatum) must be instilled to the affected nostril. The fine powder of alum with cow's ghee must be instilled into the nostrils. Sometimes the juice of Doorva grass if instilled into the nose as nasal drops will stop the bleeding soon.

Anutaila can also be used for this purpose. Internally Kooshmanda Swarasa (one ounce) with Swarana Makshika Bhasma can be given in a dose of 2-5 grs. twice daily.

A linctus prepared from Adhatoda Vasika named Vasavaleha can be given, one teaspoonful twice daily, with milk with Chandraputipravala Bhasma 200 mg.

Even Chyavanprashavaleha can also be given.

Diet: The patient is advised to take sweets, grapes, soup of green gram, meat soup, cow's milk, butter, ghee, old rice and dadima. One should not take either pungent, sour saline foods.

Other Regimens: One should not expose oneself to hot climate and indulgle in eating food which vitiates pitta and rakta. The blood pressure should be checked and if it is high, then it should be treated with Arjin tablets (Alarsin) and Siledin each one tablet three times daily. The dose can be increased when the blood pressure is high along with Sarpagandha powder 5-10 grs. or Siledin. In cases of high blood pressure, the bleeding from the nose should not be stopped immediately.

Muktha Bhasma and Pravala Pishti can be given in a dose of 200 mg. with honey twice daily. For a permanent cure of high blood pressure, a course of Dhara treatment must be undertaken. Mental and physical excitement, emotions and exercise must be forbidden.

HEADACHE

When the patient gets pain in the head it is called a headache. It is produced due to different causes and in Ayurveda this disease is known as Shira-Shoola and it is of 11 types.

Causes: Both psychological and physical causes will produce this disease. Tumour in the brain, emotional strain, prolonged overwork, high blood pressure, defective eyesight, sinusitis, exposure to excessive temperature like hot sun, hot fire, or exposure to cold, ulcers in the stomach and it may be a symptom after cold, influenza and other lung and instestinal disorders.

Signs and Symptoms of the Slaishmika Type of Headache: The patient will experience wastering in the eyes, heaviness in the head and inflammation in the middle ear and nose. This occurs usually early in the morning either in winter or in the rainy season, or immediately after fever in children (up to 12 years). Pittaja (bilious) type of headache will have a peculiar symptom of burning sensation all over the head and sometimes it is associated with bleeding from the nose. It is commonly aggravated during summer, autumn and midday. The headache due to vitiated vata will be almost and always associated with dryness and roughness of the eyes, sleeplessness, giddiness and different types of pains of the head.

ARDHAVABHEDAKA (HEMICRANIA)

The pain occurs on one side of the head which will be very severe in nature.

SOORYAVARTA (MIGRAINE)

It is a type of headache which starts early in the morning and goes on increasing with the sunrise. It will be maximum at midday and then taper; during the evening the pain will completely stop as soon as the sun sets.

ANANTA VATA

The patient will have a headache, which is very severe, and it will occur on the back of the head and spread from the occipital to the temporal regions.

SHANKHAKA

The headache will be confined to the temporal region only. There will be a reddish swelling in this region and it will obstruct the brain and the neck. The patient may not live for more than 3 days if it is not treated properly.

Treatment: Anutaila is in drops. It is medically prepared and is used as nasal drops. Ten drops may be instilled into each nostril. In the kaphaja type of headache, Laxmi Vilasa Rasa can be given in a dose of 1-2 tablets (0.25 gms. each) twice or thrice daily with honey or the juice of wet ginger.

In the vataja type of headache, Shring Bhasma (horn of deer), Godanti Bhasma (Calcium Sulphate), are specially burnt and Bhasma is prepared. These should be mixed with honey and ghee and administered twice or thrice daily in a dose of 0.25 gms. each.

Suvarna Suta Shekara is the choice drug in Sooryavarta, Ardhavabhedaka and Shankaka. It contains the Survarna Bhasma. It should be given in a dose of 200-400 mgs. with sugar, honey and ghee on an empty stomach along with Pravala Pishti, 200 mg.

The Pathyadi Quatha in a dose of one ounce must be administered with an equal quantity of water as a laxative. In resistant cases Shirobasti, Shirodhra and Panchakarma methods will help to cure the patient.

Diet: Old rice should be given with the extract of Kulattha (Dolichos biflorus), cow'smilk, butter and ghee are best to be used in this condition. The patients of headache must avoid pungent and fried foods.

Other Regimens: The patient who has a headache due to kapha must not expose himself to either cold weather, or cold climate. The mental causes which produce mental strain must be avoided totally. He should not sleep during the day or awaken at night. This holds good in other types of headaches also.

MYOPIA OF THE EYE

Myopia is generally named for refractive defects. It is one of the refractive defects like hypermetrophia and astigmatism. Eyesight is due to the rays of the light of the object transmitted on the retina of the eyes of the observer through the lens. This sensation will be carried to the brain by a pair of optic nerves. The visual defects are very common especially in young age. The patient may be heading for progressive myopia if he starts using concave lens, hence, this must be corrected by some methods which are advocated in Ayurveda. This is called "Drishti Dosha" in Ayurveda.

Causes: The common causes for myopia are due to seeing objects which are dazzling on the screen in a cinema house or due to defective reading. Ayurveda says that persons suffering from Purana Pratishyaya (chronic cold) and constipation are likely to become myopic. Vata vitiation may also lead to this disorder.

Signs and Symptoms: The patient will feel difficulty in reading and he will have a blurred vision of the objects written on the screen or on the blackboard. He may find it difficult to recognise a person at a short distance. He may notice watering in the eyes, heaviness in the head and burning sensastion in the eyeballs and attains loss of sleep and headache.

Treatment: Treating the cause is the best treatment. He must be given a laxative like Triphala-60 grains or 1 teaspoonful at bedtime with honey and ghee to prevent constipation. Cold decoction which is prepared by adding 150 ml. of water to one gram of Triphala powder filtered in the morning should be used for internal purpose for washing the eyes. Madhuyashti can also be given internally with ghee and honey. Patoladi Ghrita, Mahatriphaladi Ghrita (half to one ounce at bedtime with milk) and Saptamrita Loha 200 mg. BD with honey are some of the important drugs used in correcting visual defects. Eye exercises like sunning, palming, swinging, candlelight reading, playing with the ball and applying cold pad to eyes, must be adopted.

Sunning: The patient should aply Resolvent-200 with a glass rod to each eye; after sitting he should face the sun or a 200 watts bulb with his eyes closed and chin raised and he should sway his body side to side just like a pendulum for 5-10 minutes.

(Resolvent, 450 grms honey, 5 drops Rasanjana)

Palming: It is a method of sitting comfortably with eyes closed covered by one's palms with fingers crossed on his forehead and the elbows rested on a cushion. One should see that there should not be any pressure on the eyeball. He should see a black field before the eyes, with this the patient will feel the relief of pain and improvement of eyesight. One should avoid hurry, worry, and anxiety. If the patient has a chronic cold that should be treated properly with nasal drops like Shadbindu Taila and internally Agastya Hareetaki Tasayana (one teaspoonful) with Vasarishta (one teaspoonful with water) twice daily. The above line of treatment is very popular in our institution.

Diet: One should avoid sour, pungent foods, pickles, curd potato and other food materials which produce gas, constipation and nasal congestion. Cow's milk with cow's ghee is the best for this disorder.

Other Regimens: One should avoid seeing objects or reading continuously for a long period. One should not stay awake at night at any cost. The eye exercises which have been already mentioned must be followed strictly.

OTORRHOEA

The ear is a very important organ as it helps human beings to hear outside sounds. It has got three portions: Internal ear, Middle ear and the External

Bakula (Lat. Mimus ops Elergi)

ear. The middle ear is linked with Nasopharynx through the eustachian
tube. The inflammation that occurs in the ear is called otitis.If it occurs

in the external ear it is known as external otitis. Due to the inflammation, pus will form and will come out through the tympanic membrane through the external ear. This condition is known as Otorrhoea. In Ayurveda this disease is called 'Pootikarna'.

Causes: It is produced due to the vitiation of kapha and vatadosha, sometimes due to pitta doshas. Many a time it is also produced due to chronic cold, cough and inflammation of the sinus. It is very common in children, though rare in adults.

Signs and Symptoms: The child will notice pus coming from the ear associated with a foul smell and severe pain. The child will start crying now and then with this condition. It will be associated with fever, cough and cold. Kapha dosha is the major root cause for this disorder.

Nirgundi Nasal Drops: This is prepared from vitex-nirgundo; the juice of the leaves of this plant should be added with Sarshapa Taila (mustard oil) and boiled till the taila is retained. This oil is to be instilled into the affected ear twice daily. Triphala Guggulu to be given in a dose of ½ tablet per day.

Diet: One should avoid food which aggravates kapha like curd, sour fruits, bananas, excessive fluid or sweets, and fruits and exposure to cold atmosphere.

Other Regimens: One should avoid exposing one's body to cold. The patient should not take a cold bath, cold foods, and avoid injury to the external ear. Exposing the ear to loud sounds should be avoided.

PYORRHOEA

Pyorrhoea is a disease that affects the gums and teeth. Depending upon the involvement of gums and teeth, it is classified into different types. The most common variety is Pyorrhoea Alveolaris. There will be inflammation of the dental-periosteum, with necrosis of the alveoli resulting in the looseness of the teeth. In Ayurveda this is called "Upakusha".

Causes: If a person does not clean his teeth regularly and so also his mouth after intake of food, it may also result in pyorrhoea. It also is due to irregularity in digestion and constipation.

Treatment: One should apply ginger, pepper, rock salt, honey and ghee; this can be used for gargling also after making it warm along with oil. One should brush the teeth with any one of the sticks of Khadira, Bakula and Arjuna. In order to remove constipation Triphala powder should be given, one teaspoonful with milk at bedtime.

Data Dhavana Churna (DDC): The major ingredients are Bakula, Khadira, Sphatika, Tankana, Triphala, Laksha, Babbula and Saindhava Lavana, or G.32 tablets of Alarsin Company can be used for brushing the teeth as well as for gargling of the mouth.

Diet: Sweet foods are not to be used. Apples, pomegranates, Amalaki and guava should be given to the patient. The Amalaki contains Vitamin C in abundant quantity. Vegetables which have a bilter taste like Patola, Karavella and Shigru are very useful. Shigru leaves contain Vitamin 'A' in large quantities.

11

RHEUMATIC ARTHRITIS AND ITS REMEDIES

RHEUMATISM

Rheumatism is a disorder associated with pain and swelling in the joints and muscles. It is called Amavata in Ayurveda. Persons who are in the habit of consuming food which has antagonistic properties with indigestion will produce Ama. And if a person exercises immediately after the intake of fatty food, it will also lead to the production of Ama, in later stages it will be shifted to the joints.

Signs and Symptoms: The patient will notice swelling, fever and pain in the joints and the inability to move a particular leg, arm or both. The patient will have pain all over the body, loss of taste in the food, thirst, lethargy, heaviness in the body, fever and indigestion. The pain in the joints will first start from the lumbosacral region. If not treated, it will spread on to the joints of the legs and arms. The patient will feel a sense of pain, which will resemble the pain caused due to a scorpion bite. The patient will also have symptoms such as indigestion and mental disturbance.

Treatment: The juice of Guduchi in a dose of one ounce twice daily with 10 grains of dry ginger powder can be given. Either Yogaraja Guggulu or Mahayograj Guggulu or Simhanada Guggulu can be administered internally in a dose of two tablets twice daily with hot water. All the above prescriptions contain Guggulu (Balsamodendron mukul), a gum resin obtained from tree, Cumifora mukul. It is abundantly grown in Gujarat and Rajasthan. In research made at the Banaras Hindu University, it is proved to have anti-inflammatory and anti-arthritic properties. The fresh one will promote growth and fatness in the body, whereas the old one will produce a reverse effect that is required in

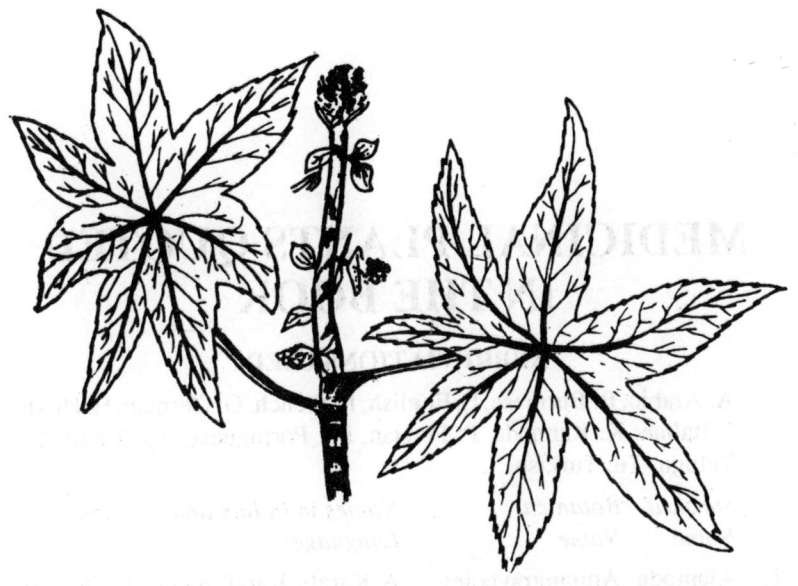

Eranda (Lat. Ricinus communis)

rheumatism. It also reduces the cholestrol. This is adopted in Medo-Roga, ever since Sushruta's period. So it is also very beneficial for hypertensive patients. If rheumatism is not treated in the early stages it affects the joints and ultimately the heart, so one should take prompt treatment in the initial stage itself.

External Application: Amavatahari Taila (Imcops, Madras), can be applied or Kottunchukadi Taila (Arya Vaidya Pharmacy, Coimbatore). It must be applied very slowly. It can also be used for massaging other parts of the body. Eranda Ksheera Paka is found to be very beneficial in this disease also.

Diet: The patient should be made to remain on fasting or on a light gruel diet. Sour things, curd and pulses must be completely forbidden. Here among the pulses the exception is green gram. One should not take cold and fried things.

Other Regimens: The patient must be allowed to take limited physical exercise. One should avoid sleeping during the day, night vigil and drinking cold water, cold bath and exposure to cold atmosphere.

MEDICINAL PLANTS QUOTED IN THE BOOK

ABBREVIATIONS USED

A: Arabic, B: Burmese, E: English, F: French, G: German, H: Hindi, I: Italian, K: Kannada, P: Persian, Po: Portuguese, Ta: Tamil, Te: Telugu, Tu: Turkish.

Sanskrit Name	Botanical Name	Names in Indian and Foreign Languages
1. Ajamoda	Apiumgraveoles	A-Karafs, Karafs nabati, E-Clery, F-Achedesmarais celeri, Ache, G, Echter sellerie, Cellerie, H-Ajawan, I-Appo, Acciosedeuo, Seleno Ajawan, K-Omu, P-Karasb, Po-aipo, Ta Omam, Te-omamu, Tu-keroviz.
2. Amlika	Tarmarindus indica	A-Umbli, Tamrhindi, B-Magi, E-Tamarind-tree, F-Tamariueer, Tamarin, G-Tamarinde, Tamarin denbaumm, H-Emli, I-Tamarundo dolce, K-Hunase Hannu, p- Ambalah, Tamarindi, Po-Tamarindo hinding, Ta-Ambilam, Te-Chintapandu, Tu-Temir hinding, Hind hurmasi,Termar.
3. Ashoka	Sarala asoca	B-Thawgabo, E-Ashoka, H-Kohah, Ta-Marudai, Te-Yarramaddi.
4. Aswa-gandha	Withania somnifera	H-Asagandha, Ta-Amukkirakalangu, kalalngu gandha Te Pannerugadda.
5. Aluka	Solanum tuberosum	E-Potato, K-Alugadde, P-Batala.

6. Amkala Emblica- A-Amlag, Assana nir, B-Hziphyus
officinalis habju, E-Emblic myrobalan, F-
Eblique officinal, G-Grane
Myobalane, H - Amvala, I-
Mirobalano embelica, K-Nallikayi,
P-Amelah Amuleh, Ta-Nellakaru,Te-
Usarikay, Tu-Amlac.

7. Amra Mangifera indica B-Thayet, E-Mango, F-Manguier,
Ariredemango, G-Mangobaum, I-
Mangiferadomune, K-Mavu, P-
Amba, Ambeh, Naghyak, Po-Manga,
Tu-Manguag Hindikirazaz, Ta-
Mamara, Te-Mamidi.

8. Babbula Acacia Arabica

9. Bala Sidacordifolia H-Kikar,K-Gobbalimara,
Takaruvel,Te-Nallatumma.

10. Bhindika Hiniscus E-Ladyfinger, Hindi Kannada
esculentus Bendekayi, Malayalam

11. Bringaraja Ecliptaaba A-Suweyd, E-Trailing Eclipta, F
Ecliptedroite, G-Aufrechte
mehlblume, H-Bhangara, I-Eclipta,
K-Garugada Soppu, Po-Surucaina,
Ta-Kayikeshi, Te-Galagara, Tu-
Kiazib paskalyacic.

12. Bhumya- Phyllanthusniruri B-Miziphiyu, F-Harbeduchagrin, G-
malaki Wilsse blattblume, Hindi-
Bhuiamvala, K-Nelanalligida, Po-
Quebrapedra Ta-Nillanelli, Te-
Nelalusarika.

13. Bibhitaki Termina A-Balilag, Balilah, B-Bankha, E-
liabelerica Belerica myrobalan, F-E-
Belerricmyrobalan, G-Myrobala-
neubaum, H- Baheda, I-MIrobalano,
K-Tarekayi,P-Balola,Ta-akkadam,
Te-Tadikayi, Tu-Balilac.

14. Bilva Aegle marmelos A-Bull, Quithtelh ind, B-Okshit,
opeshit, E-Bael Tree, F-Beliudieu,

G-Bhelbaum, H-Bael, I-Bellaindiana, K-Bilpatre, P-Safarjale hindi, TaVilvam, Te-Bilvamu, Tu-ayvaag.

15. Bimbi   Coccina indica   A-Kabarhindi, B-Kenbung, E-Scarlet fruited Gourd, F-Coccinie, G-Scharlachrank, H-Kundaru, I-Coccolabauvifera, K-Tondekayi, P-Kabaret hindi, Ta-Kobayi, Te-Dontega, Tu-Kironizl hindi.

16. Brahmi Cantella asciatica   H-Brahmi, K Ondelaga, Ta-
    and Baco-   Vallarikiri, Te SarawatiAku.
    pamonnieri

17. Dadima   Punigrantaum   A-Rumman, Allufa, B-Salebiu, Talibin, E-Polmegranate, F-Grenaadier,G-Echter Granatabaum, I-   H-Anar,   I-Pomegrantate pomopunico, K-Dalimbehannu, P-Anar, Po-Roma, Ta-Madalai, Te-Darimma, Tu-Narag.

18. Durva   Cybodon   A-Nigilnager, Thil, E-Scutgrass,
             dactylanlina   Harialiconch grass, F-Huberdu bermudes,   Chiendeut,   G Schtahundrzahn, H-Doobh, I-Dentecanino,   Capriola,   K-Garikehullu,Po-Capim deburro,Ta-Arugamapillu, Te-Door-valu, Tu-Buyukarikotu.

19. Eranda   Ricinus   A-Khirwa, B-Kesu, E-Castor oil plant,
             communis   F-Ricin, Palma, Christi, G-Echter Wunderbaum Palma, Christi, H-Echter Wunderbaum Palme Christie, H-Erandi, K-Haralugida, P-Bedangir, Po-Mamona, Ta-Amanakku, Te-Amidapuchettu, Tu-Beydencir,Harra, Hint Geneotu.

20. Godhuma Triticum   E-Wheat, H-Gehu, K-Godhi, Ta-Te
             destivam

21. Gokshura   Tribules terratris   H-Gokharu, K-Neggila Mullu, Ta-Nerunaji, Te-Pannerumullu.

22. Guduchi   Tinosphora cordifolia   H-Giloy, K-Amritaballi, Ta-Shindal kodi, Te-Tippatige.

23. Guggulu   Commiphora mukul   H-Gugal, K-Guggula, Ta-Gukkala, Te-Maishakshi.

24. Gunja   Abrus precatorius   H-Ratti, K-Gulugunji, English Indian Liquorice. Po-Tento pequeno, Ta-Mani, Te-

25. Haridra   Curumalonga   A-Aquid hindi, kurkum, B-Hsan wen Tannu, E-Tumeric, F-Curcuma Sofrandes indes, G-Gilburirzei, H-Haldi, I-Curcumalunga, K-Arasina, P-Darzardi, Ta-Manchal, Te-Pasupa, Tu-Kurkum.

26. Haritaki   Terminaliachebula   A-Shagar, Shir hindi, B-Pangah, E-Chelublic Myrobalan, F-Myrobalan chebula, G-Rispigu, Myrobalan eubaum, H-Hard, I-Mirobalano nero, K-Alahkekayi, Ta-Kandakayi, Te-Karakayi, Tu-Kabalihalile.

27. Hingu   Ferula foetida   A-Angudar, Shagabukabir, E-Asafoetida, F-Assafoet ida, G-Asandisteckenkavat, H-Hing, I-Assafoetida, K-Hingu, F-Assafoetica, Ta-Perungayam, Te-Inguva, Tu-Slytanboku.

28. Ikshu   Saccharum officinarum   A-Qassals essukkar, Qussals, B-Kyan, Keyan, E-Sugarcane, F-Canneasucre cannamella, G-Zuckerrohr, H-Ganna, I-Cannada Zucchero, cannamellae-zucchero, cannamele, K-Kabbux, P-Naishakar, Ta-Ikku, Te-Cheraku, Tu-Sekar-Kamisi.

29. Isabagoi   Plantago ovata   H-Esabgol, K-Isapgol, Te-Eshappu, Ta-Esabgalu vittalu.

30. Jata-mamsi	Nardostachys jatamamsi	A-Subbulhindi, E Spikkenard, F-Nardindien, G-Indischenarde, H-Balachad, I-Spignardi, K-Jatamamsi, P-Sunbeuttib, Ta-Jatamamsi, Te-Jatamansi, Tu-Sunbulihindi.
31. Jatiphala	Myrtica fragrans	A-Gawzettib, gawzbuwa, B-Myatle, E-Nutmeg, F-Muscadier, G-Musktnussbaum, H-Jayphal, I-NocemoscataMiristica, K-Jayikayi. P-Gauzibuya, Ta-Jatikayi, Te-Jajikaya.
32. Jiraka	Carum carvi (black)	T-kucuk hindistan, Cervizag, H-Kalajira K-Kari Jeerige, Ta-Shanaji Sharege, Te-Sema Jalakara, Tu-Kucuk hinoistran.
33. Jiraka (white)	Cuminum cyminum	A-Kammun, Sannut, B-Ziya, E-Cumin seeds, F-cumin G-Echterro-merkummel, H-I-Cominodomes-tico ciminodolee, K-Sweta Jiraka, Ta-Jirakam, Te-Jelakari, Tu-cimen kimyon.
34. Kakam-achi	Solanum nigrum	A-Enabethasthalab, E-Blacknight-shade, F-Morella noire and Amourette, G-Schwarzenaschts-chatten, H-Makoji, I-Solanohero solatro orrouse and Morella, K-Garikegida, P-Rubahlareek. Ta-Kanchipundu, Te-Mannatakalipullum, Tu-Kopekuzumu.
35. Kapi-kacchu	Mucuna prurita	A-Miyukunatel boqar, B-Khuele, khwele, E-Cowage, F-Poisagratter Muwne, G-Nackfasel, Stecjendeecte fasal, H-Kaunch, I-Lagiolodi Rio Negro, K-Nasugunni Bheeja, P-Auaregharash, Po-demico, Ta-Pilli Adagu, Te-Punaikayi.

36. Kapitha Feronia limonia

A-Tuffahh kabit, B-Hman Mahan, E-Woodapple, F-Feronic delinde, G-Elephantapfel, H-kaith, I-Pomod cleflante, K-Beladamara, P-Kabit, Ta-Bilamaram, Tc-Velaga, Tu-Filelmasi.

37. Karkotika Cucumissativus

A-Khiyar Quathad, B-Thagwa, Thagwathee, E-Common cucumber, F-Concombre, G-Echte, Gurkekku-mer, H-Vanaka Kod, I-Colomeroce-triolo, K-Madivala, P-Shiyarekhurd, Po-Peipino, Ta-Paluppakka, Te-Agakara, Tu-Hiyar Fidam.

38. Katuki   Picrrohiza kurroa

A-Kharbagehindi, E-Kurroa, K-Katukarohini, Ta-Kadagur, Te-Katukarohini, P-Kharbaquehindi.

39. Karavel-   Momordica
    laka   charantia

A-Kharbagehindi, E-Kurroa, K-Hagalakayigida, P-Karelah, Po-Melao-de-sao Caetano, Ta-Pakal, Te-Karak.

40. Kesara   Crocus sativus

A-Zafaran, B-Thanwai, E-Saffron, F-Safrone, Safron cultive, G-Echter saffron, H-Nagakesar, I-Zafferano, Erocofiorito, Fiori, Forcunculo, K-Nagakesari, Ta-Villultu, T-Nagakesaramu.

41. Khadira Acacia catechu

A-Kad, Kashu, B-Sha, E-Catechu Tree, F-Catechu, Acacieaucachon, G-Katechu akazic, H-Khair, I-Acacia di cachoue, H-Kampu kaggali, Ta-Kachukatti, Te-Podalmanu, Tu-Kadhindi.

42. Koshtaki Luffaacutangula

H-Torayi, K-Kadukkahihiregid, Ta-peppirakam, Te-Varribheera.

43. Kulanjana Alpinia
              galanga

A-Khawlangan, B-Padagoji, E-Galangal, F-Galaanga Majeur, G-Galant, H-Kulanjan, I-Alpinia

Galanga Maggiore, K-Dvipantara
Baje P-Khurduwara, Ta-Geraraltayi,
Te-Peddudumpu.

44. Kulattha Dolichos biflorus   A-Qualth, Hubulkilat, E-Horsegram,
F-Dolibiflore, grain decheval, G-
pferdekonn,   H-Kulathi,   I-
Dolicocavalina, K-Huralikalu, Ta-
Te-Tu-Alboyruce.

45. Kumari Aloebarbadensis H-Pika Amr, K-Lolasara, Po-Babosa,
Ta-Kattoli, Te-Ghusamasaram.

46. Kus-   Benincasa white A-Majdabh, B-Kayauk, E-White-
manda   hispida   gourd, F-Courage Alacire, G-Wach-
skurbis Prugel Kurbis, H-Pela, I-
Zuccadellacera, K-Boodigumbala, P-
Kadurumi, Majdabh, Te-Kalayapu-
chuni, Te-Gummodi, Tu-Monkabagi.

47. Kusmanda Cucurbita   K-   H-
(Yellow)   maxima   Ta-   Te-
Tu-   Po-Abobora.

48. Kutaja Holarhena   A-Lisanel assafirel murr, B-Letong
antidysenterica kye, lettlopgyee, E-Kurchi, F-
Holarrhine anti-dysentrique H-
Kudaiya, I-Warhena, K-Kodasige,
P-Inderjave Talhk, Ta-Veppalayi, Te-
Kodisapala, Tu-Asisercedili.

49. Lasuna Allivum sativum A-Thawan, B-Kesumplin, E-Garlic,
F-Ail, G-Knoblauch, H-Lashun, I-
Aglio, P-sir, K-Bellulli, Po-Alho, Ta-
Vellulli, Te-Tellagada, Tu-Sarmusal,
Sarmisak.

50. Lodhra Symplocosra- A-Lutr, Armak, B-Dakyat, E-Lodh-
cemosa   tree, F-Lotour, lotur, lotabum, H-
Lodh, K-Lodhra, Ta-Vellilota, Te-
Tellalodukchettu,   Tu-Kurfeag
Amerikacali.

51. Mansala Psidium guajava A-Guwafah, Safra, B-Malaka, E-
Guava, F-Goyavier, G-Grossegelbe-

guayava, F-Goyavier, G-Grossegelbe-
guayava, H-I-Gaajave, P-Sidio,
perodellindie, K-M-Po-Goiaba, Ta-
Te-Malagu, Tu-Hindarmuduay.

52. Maricha Piper nigrum A-Fulfulaswad, B-Nayukon, E-
Black-pepper, F-Poivriernoir, G-
Gemeiner Pfeffer Pepenero, H-
Kalimirchi, K-Menasu, P-Pilpel, T-
Siah biber, Ta-Malagu, Te-Miriyalu.

53. Masha Phaseolus radiotus A-Mash, E-Blackgram, F-Harico-
tmungo, G-Mungobohne, H-Udad,
I-Fagiolo Azigzag, K-Uddu, P-Benu-
mash, Ta-Ulandu, Te-Minumu, Tu-
Angolafasulyasi.

54. Mathi Trigonella
foenum gracecum

55. Mridvika Vitisvinifera A-Karm Enab. B-Sabisisabjit, E-
Grape, F-Vigne, vigne noble, G-
Weinrabe, H-Munakka, I-Vite, K-
Drakshi Hannu, P-Angur, Po-uva,
Ta-Kadimandi, Te-Drakshapandu,
Tu-Aswa.

56. Mudga Phaseolus-mungo A-Mashedamy, B-Pai, Painouk, E-
Mung, F-Haricot mungo, G-
Rauhhaarigebohone, H-Mungkidal,
K-Hesarukalu, P-Mung.

57. Musta Cyperus rotundus A-Zibielmaiz, Sugaat, E-Indian-
Cyperus, F-Souchetrond, G-
Roundezyperwrzel, H-Mothaa, K-
Konnarrigadde. I-Cipero Orientale,
Padulina, P-Muskzamin, Po-Tirirca,
Ta-Koraikelangu, Te-Tungamusthi.

58. Mulaka Raphanus sativus A-Fioy Fugel, B-Moula, E-Garden
radish, F-Navetrave, G-Rettich, H-
Mooli, I-Rafano, K-Mulangi, P-
Turkhmeturub, Po-Rabanete, Ta-
Mullangi, Te-Mullangi, Tu-Turp.

59. Nagake- Mesuaferra   H-Nagakesar, K-Nagakesari, Ta-Ve
    sara   lutta champakam, Te-Nagakesaram.

60. Narikela Cocosnucifera   A-Gawzel hind, Nargil, B-Ondionti,
                              E-Cocanut, F-Cocatier, G-Indian
                              ischer Musbaum, K-Okospalme, H-
                              Narial, I-Alberodelcocco coccopalm
                              dilatte, K-Thenginakayi, P-Bading,
                              Po-coconargi, Ta-Tennamaram, Te-
                              Narikadam, Tu-Narcilag Hundustan

61. Nimbu   Citrus media   A-Tuffahhmahi, B-Shanktakera, E-
                              Adamsapple, F-Cedratier, Cedrat, G-
                              Echte zitrone, H-Neem, I-Cedre, K-
                              Beivinamara, P-Ruranj, Po-Limao,
                              Ta-Vembu, Te-Vepa, Tu-Agaceka-
                              vunuag.

62. Nirgundi Vitex nigundo   A-Aslag, B-Kiyubin, H-Samhalu, K-
                              Nilittuvina lakkigida, P-Bunjang
                              asht., Ta-Vennochi, Te-Tellavavili.

63. Palasha   Butea monos   A-Batiyah, B-Pank, pin, ponk, E-
              perma   Bastard teak, F-Butee, Arbrea lagre,
                              G-Kinobaum laikbawan, H-Dhak,I-
                              Butea, K-Muttugmara, P-Darakh-
                              tepolah, Ta-Muruk, Te-Moduga, Tu-
                              Salansacag.

64. Patola   Trichosanthes   E-Wildsnake gourd, F-Trischosauthes
              dioica   Controurue, G-Schlagen Fruchliga
                              hearblume, H-Paraval, K-Kahi Padu-
                              valu, P-Palol, Ta-kombu Padalai, Te-
                              Advipotla.,

65. Pashana   Bergenia ligulata A-Burbit, Siyof, E-Indian Rock-
    Bheda   Foilyam, F-Flamebedean, G-Wesser-
                              schwertelilie, H-Pakhanbhed, I-Aco-
                              rofalso, Glado-orogiallo, K-Hittuluka,
                              Ta-Te-Pindichettu, Tu-Sarisusan,
                              Kilicotu.

66. Pippali   Piperlongum   A-Erqedhdhahabdarfuljul, B-Peik-
                              chm, E-Long pepper, F-poivrier long,

G-Longerpfeffer, H-People, I-Albero-
delpepe, pepe longo, K-Hipli, P-Pipal,
Ta-Tipli, Te-Pipul, Tu-Baferag,
darfulful.

67. Purarnava Boerhaavia diffusa A-Sabaka, E-Pigweed, F-Patgon, H-
Biskapara, K-Komme, P-Devasapat,
Ta-Sukuyuattgida, Te-Galijeru.

68. Sarpa-   Raulfia   H-Dhaval Varuva, K-Sutra Nabhi,
    gandha   serpentina   Ta-Chivana Nelapodi, Te-Patala
                               gandhi.

69. Simbi   Dolichoslablal   E-Beans, K-

70. Supari   Arecacatechu   A-Fulful Tanbul Kanshal, B-Kun,
                                 kumsi, E-Supari palm, F-Novselted
                                 inde Aerc, G-Pinangpalme, Areka-
                                 palme, H-Supari, K-Adakekayi, P-
                                 Girdchob, popal, pupal, Ta-Te-Tu-
                                 Fulfalg, Arckhurmaag.

71. Surana   Amorphophallus   H-Sooran, K-Choornagedde, Ta-
                campanulatus   Karula, Te-Mushnakanda

72. Sali   Oryzasativa   F-Ruz, B-Chan, San, E-Rice, A F-
                                 Riz, G-Rees, H-Chaval, I-Reso, K-
                                 Akki, P-Biranj, Po-Arroz, Ta-Te-
                                 Tu-Piriuc.

73. Sobhan-   Mormigaoleifera H-Sahijan, K-Nuggegida, Ta-Muru-
    jana   ngai, Te-Munga.

74. Shunti   Zingeber   A-Zagabil, B-Khyensing, E-Ginger,
                officinale   F-Gingermbre, H-Shont, K-Shunti,
                                 Ta-Shukku, Te-Shonti.

75. Tila   Sesamum indicum A-Sim, B-Hnan, E-Sesame, F-Sesame
                                 Jugeoline, G-Sesam, ollinge, H-Tila,
                                 I-Sesamo Giuggiolena, K-Ellu, Po-
                                 Kunjad, Po-Gergelim, Ta-valleneya,
                                 Te-Gubbalu, Tu-Susam, Sirlagan.

76. Trivrit   Operculina   A-Jurubud, E-Indian Japap, F-
                terpethum   Turbith, G-Turbith, H-Nishoth, I-
                                 Turbide, K-Tigadeberu, Po-

			Mechoacao, Ta-Shivadai, Te-Tegada, Tu-Tarbit.
77.	Tulasi	Ocimumsanctum	E-Hydharil, H-Tulasi, K-Tulasigida, Ta-Tulasi, Te-Gapparachettu.
78.	Varuna	Cretiva religosa	E-Three leaved caper, F-Crativier, G-Krateva, Tapiabaum, H-Baruna, K-Mattmavu, Ta-Mavilingm, Te-Urumatti.
79.	Vasa	Adhatoda vasaka	A-Adhatudah, E-Malbarnut, F-Noyerde malabar, G-Malabaris chenuss, H-Adusa, I-Justica arbonescente, K-Adusoge, M-P-Bansa, Ta-Ada Dodayi, Te-Adasaram, Tu-Malabarcevigag.
80.	Vidanga	Embeliaribes	A-Kabuli, Biring, E-Embelia, F-Ribelier, G-Embelie, H-Vayuvidanga, I-Embelia, K-Vayavidangam, P-Birange Kabali, Ta-Baybilam, Te-Vellal, Bu-Biring, Kabuli.
81.	Yastima-dhu	Glycyrrihiza glabra	A-Shag, B-Noiekhiyan, E-Liquorice, F-Reglisseglabre, G-Echtessussholz, H-Muleti, I-Regolizca, K-Atimadhura, P-Bikkhenahak, Po-Alcacuzdaeuropa, Ta-Atimadhuram, Te-Yastimadhukam, Tu-Megarkoku.
82.	Yava	Hordeum vulgare	A-Shair, B-Muyan, E-Barley, F-Orge Commune, G-Saatgerde Gerete, H-I-Oryzocommunne, K-Barli, P-Jao, Ta-Te-Tu-Arpa.

MAJOR MANUFACTURERS OF AYURVEDIC MEDICINES AND FORMULATIONS IN INDIA

1. Afali Pharmaceuticals Ltd., Ahmadnagar, Maharashtra.
2. Alarsim, 12, K.Duhasha Margi Fort, Bombay 400 023
3. Aryavaidyashala, Kottakal, Kerala.
4. Aryavaidya Pharmacy (CBE) Ltd., 366, Trichy Road, Coimbatore.
5. Baidyanath Ayurveda Bhavan, Nagpur, Patna, Calcutta.
6. Bharatiya Aushadha Nirmana Shala, Dr. V.S.Marg, Gondal Road, Rajkot.
7. Charaka Phasrmaceutical, Bombay 400 011.
8. Dhanwantari Jwala, Ayurveda Bhavan, Mamubhajua Road, Vijayagarha, Aligarh, UP.
9. Dabur (Dr.S.K.Burman), New Delhi 110 002.
10. Deccan Ayurveda Pharmacy, Hyderabad, A.P.
11. Dhootapapeswar Ltd., 135, Desai Road, Bombay 400 004
12. Gujarat Ayurveda Vikasa Mandal Bhavan, Ahmedabad 380 014
13. Gujarat Ayurveda University Pharmacy, Jamnagar 361 001
14. Govt. Central Pharmacy, Jayanagar, Bangalore, Karnataka.
15. Himalaya Drug Co., Shivasagar Dr. A. B. Road, Bombay 400 018.
16. Indian Medicine Industries, Nagalands, Vijayawada 520 004.
17. Imcops, Lattice Brigade Road, Adyar, Madras.
18. Indian Pharmaceutical Ltd., Udupi, S.Karnataka.
19. N.K.C.A.Pharmacy Pvt. Ltd., Anathalya Road, Mysore, Karnataka.
20. Orient Pharma, Indian Medicine Division, Madras.
21. Oushadi, The Pharmaceutical Corpn., of Kerala Ltd., Trichur.
22. Sadvaidya Shala Pvt. Ltd., Nanjangud, Karnataka.
23. Susi Pharmaceuticals Ltd., V.V.Mohalla, Mysore, Karnataka.
24. Swadeshi Oushada Bhandar, Kunja, Udupi, S. Karnataka.
25. Sita Raghava Vaidya Shala, P.B. No. 35, Mysore 570 001.
26. Unsha Pharmacy, Unjha, Gujarat.
27. Yogi Pharmacy, P.O. Gurukul, Kangri, Haridwar 249 404.
28. Zandu Pharmaceuticals, Ltd., Dadar, Bombay 400 025.

INDEX

ENGLISH AND AYURVEDIC EQUIVALENTS
IN BRACKETS

Anaemia (Pandu Roga)   42
Anorexia (Arochaka)   10
Asthma (Swasa Roga)   37
Amenorrhoea (Nasta Raja)   70
Black Water Fever (Kalamasha Jwara)   57
Biliary Colic (Pittashaya Shoola)   28
Bronchitis (Swasa Pranali Shotha)   36
Bulbous Eruptions (Visphotaka Jwara)   64
Cataract (Timira)   108
Chickenpox (Laghu Mashoorika)   62
Cholera (Vishoochika)   20
Conjunctivitis (Abhishyanda)   108
Cirrhosis of the Liver(Yakritvriddhi)   46
Colic Pain   25,27
Common Cold (Pratishayaya)   33
Common Fever (Jwara)   52
Constipation (Koshtabaddhata)   11
Dandruff (Arunshika)   98
Dengue Fever (Dandaka Jwara)   59
Diabetes (Madhumeha)   86
Diarrhoea (Atisara), Infantile   15
Diphtheria (Rohini)   59
Displacement of Uterus (Yoni Vyapagata)   79

Dysentery (Raktatisara, Pravahika) 19
Dyspepsia (Agnimandhya) 13
Dysuria (Mutrakrichra) 67
Epistaxis (Urdhwaga Rakta Pitta) 110
Eczema (Pama) 93
Epilepsy (Apasmara) 102
Erysipelas (Visarpa) 65
Fevers (Jwara) 52
Filaria (Sleepada) 56
Gonorrhoea (Ushnavata) 77
Goiter (Gala Ganda) 92
Gout (Vata Rakta) 91
Greying of Hair (Palitya) 97
Haematemesis (Urdhwaga Rakta pitta) 27
Haemoptysis (Urdhwaga Raktapitta) 39
Haematuria (Adhoga Rakta Pitta) 68
Haemorrhage (Raktapitta) 48
Headache (Shira Shoola) 111
Heat Exhaustion (Anshughata Jwara) 61
Heat Stroke (Anshughata Sannipata) 61
Hectic Fever (Pralepaka Jwara) 58
Hiccough (Hikka Roga) 34
Hoarseness of Voice 39
Hypochlorhydria (Annadrava Shoola) 27
Hypertension (Raktavata) 48
Hysteria (Yoshapasmara) 101
Impotency (Klaibya) 85
Influenza (Vata Sleshmaka Jwara) 34
Insomnia (Nidranasha) 105
Jaundice (Kamala) 44
Kala Azar (Kala Jwara) 57
Leucoderma (Kilasa) 94
Leucorrhoea (Sweta Pradara) 73
Leukaemia (Vatolbana Sannipataja Pandu Roga) 51
Loss of Memory (Smriti Brahmsa) 100
Low Blood Pressure (Nyuna Raktachapa) 50

Malaria	55
Measles (Romantika)	62
Meningitis (Mastishka Shotha)	58
Menorrhagia (Rakta Pradara)	71
Metrorrhagia (Adhogata Rakta Pitta)	71
Migraine (Sooryavarta)	112
Mumps	61
Myopia of the Eye (Dristi Dosha)	113
Obesity (Medoroga)	89
Otorrhoea (Pooti Karna)	114
Piles (Arshas)	30
Psoriasis (Ekakusta)	95
Puerperal Fever (Sootika Jwara)	78
Pyorrhoea (Upakua)	116
Rheumatic Fever (Amavata Jwara)	54
Rheumatism (Amavata)	118
Ringworm (Dadru)	98
Schizophrenia (Unmada)	106
Sand-fly Fever (Marumakshika Jwara)	60
Sciatica (Grudhrasi)	104
Scurvy (Shetada)	47
Smallpox (Masoorika)	62
Sprue Syndrome (Sangrahani)	21
Sterility (Vandhyatva),	80
Syphilis (Firanga Upadansha)	75
Tonsilitis (Tundiekeri)	41
Tuberculosis (Rajayakshma)	40
Thirst (Thrishna)	22
Typhoid Fever (Antrika Jwara)	53
Ulcers of the Stomach (Annadrava Shoola Parinamalashoola)	25
Vomiting (Chhardi)	24
Urinary Calculi	73
Urticaria (Sheeta Pitta)	96
Whooping Cough (Dhustakasa or Kukkasa)	35
Yellow Fever (Peeta Jwara)	60